101 Reasons *Not To* Own A Dog

Cautionary tales with some swearing and cats.

Paul Meade

Copyright © Paul Meade 2021

Paul Meade has asserted his moral right to be identified as the author of this work.

All rights reserved.

No part of this book may be reproduced, or stored in a retrieval system, or transmitted in any form or by any means, electronic, mechanical, photocopying, recording, or otherwise, without express written permission of the publisher.

First published in 2021

For Mom, Dad, June and Mary, with love.

AUTHOR'S NOTE

The idea for this book and its title came from Mike and Bev Arnold many moons ago. They have provided many of the stories; Jock the Boerboel and Captain the Jack Russell were their dogs. Dave Moberly wrote the rough draft for the chapter on Benj, the giant Boerboel, who hated going to the vet; Tibane and Dot were his dogs. Henk Coetsee told me the Cruiser story. This small book grew from the seven short articles I wrote under the same title for our local community newspaper, Nix M@tters. Dog stories are a dime a dozen; everybody has one. All the dogs included in this book are mine, were mine or are dogs I have known personally.

CHAPTERS

Chapter 1   Jock

Chapter 2   Tarn

Chapter 3   Tarn's Ladies

Chapter 4   Strike & Skyler

Chapter 5   Paul's biting dog

Chapter 6   Turk

Chapter 7   Grip

Chapter 8   Ziggy

Chapter 9   Benj

Chapter 10 Tibane & Dot

Chapter 11 Fuck Off Buddy

Chapter 12 Socks

Chapter 13 Eastwolds Farm

Chapter 14 Orla

Chapter 15 Jango

Chapter 16 Jack Russells

Chapter 17 Cruiser

Chapter 18 Kirkman Crescent

Chapter 19 Cats

Chapter 20 New Dogs

Chapter 21   Close Encounters

Chapter 22   Bees and Snakes

Chapter 23   Disclaimer

Chapter 24   101 Reasons Not to Own A Dog – The List

Chapter 25   Dog Bytes

CHAPTER ONE

JOCK

Jock was of mixed breed, but predominantly Boerboel; cream coated with a black mask, he was a tall, long-bodied, male entire. He belonged to a dairy farmer friend of mine. Mike was one of three local dairymen who trained for the Comrades Marathon by pounding the district roads around their farms. Jock was in his prime and very fit and would accompany the joggers, always trotting just ahead of them. He had a docked tail that did nothing to hide the biggest pair of shiny black nuts and an embarrassingly massive black pope's nose that pulsated as he ran. One day after weeks of training and many hours of staring at Jock's throbbing baboon-like behind, Mike's neighbour commented dryly that he could no longer stand been winked at by a dog's bum for mile on end and that either he or Jock would have to stay home.

Mike Arnold's son was four years old when he walked into the house carrying a kitten, which he proudly presented to Mike. Not wanting a cat, Mike gently told him to put it back where he found it. 'In Jock's mouth?' Tyrone asked his father incredulously.

A few years later, the Arnold's came home to find Jock painted green. When they tracked down the culprit and asked their youngest daughter why she had painted the dog, Jessica's only answer was, 'I don't care, Jock eated my bunny.' All three Arnold children had been given pet rabbits, housed in a sturdy hutch in the garden. They lasted about a week. Jock was transfixed by the rabbits and stationed himself outside the cage, spending hours watching their every move, his head darting from side to side like a laser-guided gun.

It must have been a harrowing experience for the bunnies; this notwithstanding, and clearly not being the brightest of animals, they spent all their waking hours trying to escape from the hutch and eventually succeeded. Small pieces of leftover rabbit littered the lawn. From then on, whenever a rabbit was spotted on the farm, the kids would earnestly identify them as one of their pets who had escaped Jock's jaws. One of the rabbits was black, and Mike saw no evidence of his demise in the detritus Jock had left behind. A year or so later, he was walking to the dairy in the dark, and a black rabbit nearly gave him a heart attack by brushing against his foot and darting away. Sooty had indeed survived the massacre.

CHAPTER TWO

TARN

Tarn was my first dog as an adult. As with most first dogs, he was a legend. Tarn was a three-quarter Bull Mastiff, purchased for R35 in 1981 after seeing a smalls advert in our local daily newspaper, the Natal Witness. His mother was a big dog with a large dome-shaped skull and sad eyes; she was thin and worn out from rearing a large litter of puppies. His father was not on view, having recently taken on a train head-on, snarling right to the end, according to his owner.

Tarn and I were inseparable; he went everywhere I went and slept inside the house every night, usually on my bed. He was a proper one-man dog; he barely tolerated friends and did not abide strangers. He survived being caught in a wire snare and at least one vehicular collision. A legend in his own lifetime, he sired most of the litters in our valley for a couple of years. I came home from a two-month army camp to find the dog wrapped in a makeshift wire harness chained to a pole on my front verandah. Lonely at my absence, he started following my maid MaDlamini home at night (she lived on the other side of the farm) and either killed or maimed all the male dogs he encountered on the way. The rightfully aggrieved dog owners warned her that they would kill him if she didn't stop him from following her. MaDlamini, ever-resourceful, made a plan and probably saved his life.

Tarn's transgressions were serial, and if the 101 Reasons were a test, he would have passed summa-cum-laude. He once ate a whole pot of soup straight off my employer's stove, where it had been warming up for our supper. He consumed all but the head and legs of a dead bull calf in one night of gorging. Accidently locked in the house one day, he chewed and clawed his way through a window paned door to get out. He had his pick of the couch and easy chairs. If someone sat in his favourite spot, he was not above sitting on top of them, much to the person's surprise and alarm; he was a big dog and took some moving. Looking back, I wasn't very domesticated at the time, and I let Tarn get away with murder.

I was the dairy manager on Carisbrooke Farm of Cry the Beloved Country fame when I bought Tarn. One morning our neighbour drove into the farmyard with his two big Mastiff x Ridgeback dogs on the back of his pickup. Tiger and Ringo baled off and thrashed Tarn, who must have been a year old at the time. Six months or so later, I can't remember the time scale Bo visited again, with his dogs as always on the back of his vehicle. They jumped off, eager to assert themselves again. Tarn cleaned both dogs up and had them scrambling to get back on the truck. From then on, whenever Bo's bakkie ended up at Carisbrooke, his dogs would cower below the sides of the vehicle, with Tarn parading and growling below. Tarn was never Bo's favourite dog.

In 1982, I went to work on Olivar, a neighbouring farm. Tarn was reasonably well behaved, having to live with the resident German Shepherds, a magnificent female named Sheba and her wussy son Willis. Queen Sheba being royalty, totally ignored Tarn. After a very short introduction, Willis kept his distance. It was at Olivar that Tarn ate the soup of the stove. If Tarn couldn't find me, he would often head off back to Carisbrooke. One Friday evening, when it was my weekend off, and I was going to visit my folks in Durban, I couldn't find him. We searched high and low, calling his name repeatedly to no avail. I spent the night at Carisbrooke. Early the next morning, I found him sitting in the Kikuyu paddock below the house, looking very grumpy. He had a snapped off wire snare around his neck. I removed the noose and loaded him in the front of my little Corona 120Y, and off we went to Durban. It would not be the last time one of my dogs tangled with snares.

Tarn spent a couple of years in Durban with my parents when I worked on farms where I could not take him, but in 1987 I returned to work in the Carisbrooke valley, and so did Tarn. Tiger and Ringo were no more; two impressive Rottweilers Jody and Rusty, had replaced them. They were mother and daughter. Tarn never had a problem with the fairer sex. I lived on Carisbrooke, but the dairy was on Finchley. Tarn would get bored and come looking for me when I went to milking every morning, a distance of several kilometres. He had to cross a national road to get there. Worried he would get hit by a car, I would tie him up before I left home. His tether was a long nylon ski-rope attached to his collar.

There was a cabbage crop on Carisbrooke at the time, requiring a sizeable *togt* gang for harvesting. The workers would arrive every morning, and unbeknownst to me, one of their number would tease Tarn, safe in the knowledge that the dog was tied up. The teasing went on for a couple of weeks. Unfortunately for Tarn's tormentor, I acquired a Jack Russell puppy. One morning Jos did what puppies do; she chewed through Tarn's rope. Fortunately for Tarn's tormentor, he had a good turn of speed. He ended up across the yard, standing on the roof of one of the vehicles with Tarn baying at his heels and the rest of the *togt* gang laughing their heads off.

The older Tarn got, the more tactile defensive he became. Hence, it caused some alarm the day we found Bo's youngest son frozen on Tarn's back with his arms wrapped around the dog's neck in a moment of ill-advised affection, and Tarn standing stiff-legged emitting a rumble from deep inside his chest that sounded like hell about to erupt. We all held the pose, and Pete was extricated with only the minor loss of his dignity. I found Tarn lying dead in the middle of the front lawn one afternoon; he was eleven years old. Great hound, one mourner.

Tarn

CHAPTER THREE

TARN'S LADIES

Blaise was a purebred pedigree Bull Mastiff, bought for R350 as a mate for Tarn. A magnificent specimen with one major blind spot, she hated small dogs. The wages of sin are death, and after she had attacked and mauled my much-cherished Jack Russell Jos for the third time, she was sent to meet her maker. I arrived home late one night to find a pool of blood at every door where Jos had desperately tried to get into the house to escape Blaise's attacks. After much heart in mouth searching, I found the little Jack Russell near-death, where she had crawled under some shrubbery. Only the skills and dedicated care of Jackie Morford, our local small animal vet, saved Jos's life, not once but twice.

Kyla was also a purebred pedigree Bull Mastiff. Blaise's replacement, she cost an arm and a leg but turned out to be as ugly as sin, with a protruding bottom jaw that would have made T-Rex proud. She made up for it with a heart of gold. Kyla was run over on the highway when she followed me out unseen, late one evening when we went to sit up for cattle thieves who had hamstrung a beef cow the night before. An altogether bad night.

Despite Kyla's short life, she did leave a legacy; she had a male pup by Tarn. Tarn was getting on and must have been firing mostly blanks as Sport was the only puppy in the litter. Sport grew up with the best combination of his father's looks and his mother's temperament. Like his father, he was an evangelical watchdog with a spectacular charge that could induce on the spot religious conversion.

Unfortunately, when he was about five, I changed locations, and on the new farm, Sport started roaming. If he had just gone on his own, it might have been tolerable, but he took the whole pack with him for up to three days at a time. Sport and two of his offspring were caught in snares as a result. Miraculously all three dogs survived. Finally, early one morning, after they had been gone for three days, I woke to the sounds of heavy panting and water being lapped noisily on the front verandah. I'd had enough. Sport proved to have a bullet-proof skull. Unfortunately for him, he didn't have a bullet-proof heart. Traumatic, but once Sport was gone, all the roaming stopped.

Tegan was a Boerboel x Bull Mastiff. Her mother, Zoey, once sat on a baby. Pete and Bev looking for their small daughter, were dismayed to find her flailing under the unperturbed and seemingly unaware dog's wide behind. A cheerful red brindle with a docked tail, Tegan was a great character and talked whenever you locked eyes with her. With Sport as mate, she produced three litters of magnificent puppies – the first of them were born under my bed at Carisbrooke. Ken Woodburn wanted a pup and was a frequent visitor. One day he dropped one of the pups on its head. I told Ken he had just chosen his dog. He named his puppy Scud, and he became a legend in his own right.

The only blot on Tegan's scorecard was when she and two of her grown pups would follow Sport on his rambles. Tegan must have been ten or eleven when her back legs conked in virtually overnight, and she lost all use of them. The day I took her to the vet to be euthanised, she sat next to me in the pickup, head out the window, happy as Larry, tongue lolling and with a wet nose. I blubbed all the way home.

Tegan and Jos

CHAPTER FOUR

STRIKE & SKYLER

I kept three of Sport and Tegan's progeny, only one intentionally. Strike was a magnificent red brindle dog with a black muzzle, a huge head, and a bull chest. Dumb as a stump, he took a year to learn to jump on the back of my bakkie and another year to learn to jump off again. His size should have made him an effective watchdog, but unlike Sport and Tarn before him, he never met anyone he didn't like and would allow anybody onto the property. He did eventually learn to at least bark in the right direction. As a result of following his father, the inevitable happened. He got caught in a snare (I have had four dogs caught in wire snares, two came home wearing them, and two were found still alive after days of searching when they didn't come home), despite offering all manner of rewards, we could not find Strike.

A week later, he walked in the door, looking very forlorn, his body bent and buckled. I was so pleased to see him; I couldn't be angry. He had a deep wound over his shoulder, under one leg, and across his chest and neck, which I treated with purple spray. An hour later, when he still uncomfortable and dripping urine in little spurts, I dug my fingers into the wound and found the wire loop still attached, cut deep into the flesh. I had to run up to the dairy and get the fencing pliers to cut him free. He healed up with no after-effects, except the hair grew back white over the scar. If he hadn't got one leg through the wire loop, his thrashing would have surely throttled him. One tries not to imagine the fear and pain and the slow death of an ensnared animal.

Strike was about a year old when his mother came on heat again; he showed no interest in her. Six months later, she was back in heat; this time, Strike was very interested. I kept Tegan locked up in the house. Satisfied she was safe, I went to bed. It turned out Strike could just fit his head through the burglar guards, and in his sexual frustration, he had reached through the bars and chewed the corner off the couch. A chunk of couch big enough to make a stuffed cushion if I had been so inclined.

One breeder who brought his bitch for Strike to cover always came in an old Mercedes. After that, Strike got very excited whenever he saw a big car. Not so dumb after all. Strike went downhill very fast in his last six months; he ended up looking like one of those old lions you see on the wildlife channels, giant skull and magnificent gaunt frame. Another sad visit to the vet; he was only about eight or nine.

Two litters later, I kept Strike's full sister, Skyler. Stolen as a pup, someone must have left a door or gate open because two weeks after she disappeared, she returned home covered in ticks. A yellow brindle, she had been one of my least favourite pups, but I couldn't sell her after that. Skyler also survived being caught in a snare. She had been AWOL for a couple of days, and I had put out the word she was missing. On Christmas morning, neighbours phoned to say they could hear a dog crying in the pine forest behind their house. I shot out there, and it was not long before I heard her sad lament. I hurried towards the sound and was pleased when I heard Skyler cry again. The trees were so thick and low to the ground it was impossible to see her. I made the mistake of calling out to her; upon hearing my voice, she thought she was saved and stopped crying. It took me another thirty minutes of desperate searching before I finally found her.

A copper wire noose attached to a pine sapling had trapped her back leg just above the hock, it had already cut through the skin from her struggles, and if we had found her a few hours later, the wire would have hamstrung her. If my neighbours hadn't heard her cries, she would have surely starved to death. Overjoyed to be found, I remember her sating her hunger and thirst and then sitting on the couch, gazing lovingly at me for the rest of the day. A couple of days later, she went into toxic shock from all the tick bites she had received while snared. A trip to the vet sorted that out. Skyler lived to be eleven years old and got to sleep inside every night. Good dog.

Strike

Striker Boy!

Skyler and Joad

CHAPTER FIVE

PAUL'S BITING DOG

Red was the smallest pup in Tegan's last litter but very alert and aware of his surroundings. I swapped Red for five straws of bull semen. He grew up in Pietermaritzburg and very quickly started showing disturbing signs of over the top aggression. When he was about a year old, a colleague and I stayed the night with Red's owners, Myles and Morag van Deventer, good friends of mine. Sarel was billeted in an outside room. Early the next morning, I received a call to come and fetch him; he was too scared to leave the room after spending a sleepless night with Red snuffling and growling under the door like a latter-day Hound of the Baskervilles.

Another time after the van Deventer's had moved to the National Chicks Farm in Umlaas Road, Myles was sitting in the lounge when he heard a soft hullo at the back door. There were numerous gates to go through before reaching their house, every gate bearing a large Beware of the Dog sign because of Red. Nobody came to their home uninvited. There was a second quavering hullo. Puzzled, Myles got up to find the local vet, who had ignored all the warning signs but was now very eager to get inside the house. Red was standing next to him, bristling, his head and hackles up, his tail stiff and a menacing growl rumbling from deep inside his chest.

In an attempt to socialise Red, an unfortunate Dalmatian named Ollie was purchased. Ollie had a stressful life; Red was either his best buddy, chewing him up or vigorously bonking him. The van Deventer's were transferred to Swaziland; the dogs couldn't go along. Ollie found a good home; the incorrigible Red was a hard case and would have to be put down. With Red's older brother Strike showing the bad guys the way, I had been burgled three times. A canine hard man seemed like a good idea.

Red was as dangerous as having a loaded gun lying around, and it would have been highly irresponsible of me to allow him to mingle with the general population. I fenced off my backyard and fetched the dog. Loading him was a little scary. I used to joke that we baited the back of the bakkie with a Maltese Poodle to get him to jump inside, but that wasn't true; he actually jumped aboard with little fuss. When I got home, I reversed the bakkie up to the backyard, opened the canopy, and encouraged Red out with a fresh sheep's head (really) and padlocked the gate behind him. He would live in my backyard for the rest of his life.

Red was a terror. He didn't like eye contact, raised voices, pointed fingers, and, least of all, sticks. You could show him a twig from fifty yards, and he would go berserk. I only ever challenged him from the safe side of the fence. Unlike his mother, if you locked eyes with Red, he would offer to take your throat out. Visitors were often too scared to go to the loo because Red would stand at the back door and growl at them through the security gate. My friend's young kids all knew not to go anywhere near Paul's biting dog.

A legend for all the wrong reasons, only MaMtolo and I entered his domain. As long as you adhered to all of the above and didn't make any sudden movements, you could safely enter his space, and he would even sidle up for a pat – he was not a total psychopath. I gave MaMtolo a full briefing on how to handle the dog. The cardinal rule was that if she ever tripped and fell, she should not cry out or make a fuss, just stand up quietly and hobble away, dragging her broken leg. MaMtolo never had any problems with Red. Perhaps his bark was worse than his bite.

One Sunday evening, I felt sorry for Red, living all on his own in the back yard, so I let him in the house. I followed all protocols, and he quickly stretched out fast asleep on the floor. I fell asleep in front of the television as you do. Sometime around midnight, an electrical storm of species-ending proportions broke. The front yard dogs were whining and scratching on the door to be let in. Thick with sleep and completely forgetting Red was in the house, I let them in. Bedlam! Strike couldn't believe his luck; here was the grumpy bugger who lived in the backyard at his mercy. (Strike's security skills may have been lacking, but he loved a good scrap; he once pulled Red over the top of the stable door by the scruff of his neck). In the middle of the night, with the lights flashing on and off because of the storm, I had two large dogs fighting inside the house, one of whom didn't react well to discipline. The other dogs, delightful creatures that they are, were darting in for a snack of Red whenever they could sink their teeth into an exposed part of him. I managed to get the peripheral hounds out of the house, slipped a belt around Strike's hips, and dragged him to an internal security gate, with Red still attached to the sharp end. I had a dog on either side of the gate and tried to squeeze it shut on their muzzles. To no avail; they would not let go. We were testing an aerosol paint to mark cows at the time, so I blasted this into their nostrils, and they finally parted. For the next couple of weeks, I had two green-headed bull mastiffs licking their wounds.

Red lived next to a hundred strong flock of free-range Rhode Island Reds chickens, an embryonic poultry enterprise, and the sure path to my first million. A four-foot-high fence separated chickens and dog. From time to time, you would glance out the kitchen window, and a depressed fowl, possibly high on laying mash, would fly over the fence. The kamikaze chickens flew unerringly into Red's waiting jaws, and he would consume them whole. In one particularly suicidal month, his turds started looking like owl pellets. With Red's strict culling practices, we fast-tracked Darwin, and in no time, were down to the nucleus of a new breed of entirely flightless fowl. Unfortunately, the trauma of seeing their flock mates devoured by the next-door neighbour seemed to interfere with their egg-laying, and they all ended up in the pot, as did my dreams of becoming a poultry millionaire.

In 2002, I had four dogs – Red the maladjusted, poultry munching bull mastiff living in solitary confinement in the backyard; the front garden contained Skyler, Red's sister from a previous litter, Joad, a German shepherd, and Rizzo, a sharp young Jack Russell. Joad was a seven-eighths German shepherd, one eighth timber wolf; I purchased him in Mooi River as an early warning system for the dozy mastiffs. A good looking intelligent dog, Joad's ears had started out on top of his head in the conventional five-to-one pose of all alert, sharp-nosed dogs. Strike rearranged them for him one day, and Joad became more of a quarter-past-eleven dog. Joad's life improved considerably, and he probably danced a canine jig when Strike moved on to the great dog patch in the sky.

Taking the hounds for a walk one day, I noticed Skyler was even slower and out of breath than I was. I decided younger reinforcements were needed. Barkly was a fat, biscuit coloured Boerboel pup. She grew into a powerful, slightly goofy young dog, and I loved her. I didn't realise her goofiness hid a darker side. I was in Mooi River after two days on the road and had been out of cell range all morning. Ten missed calls told me something was wrong. Sadly so. While I was away, Barkly had come on heat for the first time and killed Rizzo, the little Jack Russell. My loss was great, but in the spirit of the new South Africa, a criminal act that would have previously resulted in the death penalty was reduced to life imprisonment. I pushed Barkly out the back door to join Red. I was so angry and heartbroken over Rizzo's loss that it was months before I could bring myself to forgive her, let alone give her a pat. On the other hand, Red was overjoyed – poor chap; he didn't know what he was in for.

If there is such a thing as karma (there isn't), Red became its victim. The dog who struck fear into the hearts of all who crossed his path, who had so abused Ollie the Dalmatian at his first home, who twice put Morag up against the fence when she tried to shoo him out her veggie garden, who had eaten so many chickens he thought he lived next to a KFC and who liked to mark his territory by peeing on my gumboots, had met his match. Barkly made Red's life hell. We would hear explosions from the backyard, and it would be Barkly beating Red up for some infringement on his part. Barkly was as big as Red, heavier in fact, and in her prime. What heaped misery on Red was that his prison mate cycled like clockwork and would come into heat every six months or so. I started feeling sorry for him. The old boy would climb aboard, but though the spirit was willing, the body was not. Red had scored a trophy wife, but he could no longer get it up. It must have been purgatory.

With Bonnie and Clyde in the backyard, one would have thought I had a secure home. No such luck. The crooks used a sledgehammer to spread the burglar guards and pushed a small child (according to the fingerprint guy) through a narrow window on the side of the house the backyard dogs couldn't protect. A camera and all my clothes were stolen (my geyser had recently exploded drenching my cupboards, so all my clobber had been washed and ironed and stacked in the spare bedroom.) An internal security gate stopped the latter-day *Artful Dodger* from entering the rest of the house. I subsequently moved the fence and walled up the offending window.

Red was textbook dominance aggression, hardcore until the very end; he growled and bristled at me when I yelled at him for mock charging and scattering some sheep we were driving past his spot (another short-lived get rich quick scheme.) Just two days later, I found him dead at the back door. He was twelve years old. As aggressive as Red was, he never succeeded in biting anyone; we managed the bugger well.

With Red gone, Barkly was paroled into the front yard. Turk, who had taken over from Strike as the alpha male, knocked her up almost immediately, and within a few months of her release, she produced six pups. I kept one puppy from that litter, the mighty Grip. Due to a lapse on my part, Barkly was soon pregnant again. Overnight, Barkly delivered two pups in a hole she had dug at the bottom of the garden. We moved her onto the front verandah, and over the course of the day, she produced another three pups. That evening I heard scraping sounds from her box and thought she was just getting comfortable. When the strange sounds persisted, I went and investigated. I found Barkly standing in the middle of the verandah, her legs splayed and her eyes bulging. She appeared to be choking. As I watched, she staggered sideways into the wall and fell over. I opened her jaws; her gums and tongue were blue. I stuck my hand down her throat as far as it would go, expecting to pull out afterbirth or a dead puppy, but there was nothing there. In seconds she was dead; punching her chest and blowing into her lungs could not revive her. I looked in her box; there were now six pups, the last one still wet, was stillborn. Stunned, I found a cardboard box, put a towel in the bottom, and added the five live puppies. I put the box in the spare bedroom, covered it with a towel, and closed the door, so I wouldn't be able to hear them if they cried and decided that if they were still alive in the morning, I would do something.

They survived the night; I went onto the internet and googled orphan puppy instructions. I managed to purchase everything I needed in Ixopo. Between MaMtolo and I, we successfully hand-reared all five puppies (I did night shift and weekends.) We had to put them in separate boxes after feeds; otherwise, they would latch onto each other's extremities (wieners and fannies) and suckle until they were raw. It was hard work, so I fast-tracked their training and taught them to lap asap. The smallest pup, a little brindle female with large round eyes, was slow on the uptake and still had to be bottle-fed ten days after her littermates were noshing milky Pronutro on their own. Sucker that I am, I kept her and called her Gooch. Sadly, Gooch did not have a happy ending.

The killer hounds – Barkly and Red

Snowdogs

CHAPTER SIX

TURK

In March 2005, I owned six dogs, Skyler, Red, Barkly, Turk, a Jack Russell pup named Taz, and a seven-year-old German Shepherd called Joad, who was one eighth timber wolf and smarter than all the Mastiffs put together – somebody has to point them in the right direction. Turk was my fifth mastiff male after Tarn, Sport, Strike, and Red. He was actually half Mastiff, half Boerboel. Turk reminded me a lot of Strike. He was a little taller, not quite as broad; he had the same colouring, thick neck, big head, and deep sump of a chest. He had a beautiful silky soft coat. Unlike Strike, he had a docked tail. As a young dog, he was a happy, well-socialised animal and master of all he surveyed. The rise of his son would change that. Dominance hierarchy is not for sissies and can be heart breaking.

Turk would eat very little or possibly not eat at all when I was away and would subsequently gorge himself when I got home. One evening I got back to be greeted by all the dogs as usual. A few hours later, I noticed Turk was missing. I grabbed a torch and went looking for him. I found him at the bottom of the garden, in extremis. He was standing stock-still, weird eyed, splay-legged, severely bloated, and grunting in pain. I managed to get him into the back of the bakkie. I took him to the local vet who lived in Creighton. The young vet diagnosed his condition as gastric dilation and volvulus (stomach torsion) but informed me she did not have the tools to perform the necessary operation to relieve it. I needed to get him through to the Hilton Veterinary Clinic post-haste, or he would die. Hilton was over an hour's drive away. The whole time we were making the necessary phone calls to organize the emergency surgery, the bakkie shuddered on its wheels with a highly distressed Turk attempting to chew his way out of the fibreglass canopy. It sounded like a caged lion trying to escape.

When I stopped at the Bulwer T-junction to check on him, he managed to squeeze himself out the small side window and landed hard on the tarmac. I put him in front with me. I arrived at the clinic at midnight; Turk was lying upside down in the passenger side footwell. I thought he was dead. I opened the door, and he fell out, still grunting. Two lady vets operated on him. They had to stick a tube down his throat during the operation. Despite using their biggest pipe, they could still smell gas escaping and realised his throat was so big the pipe was not sealing it. They had to pack gauze around it to affect a proper seal. Against all the odds, under their expert care, Turk made a full recovery.

I had Turk for a decade; he was born in July 2004 and died in December 2014. He had eight good years until Grip usurped him as alpha male. They had started fighting almost every time I drove up the drive. I hated it and would always quickly part them. One day at my wit's end, I decided to let the fight take its course so dominance could be established once and for all – a bad decision. Grip's tooth went through the soft spot above Turk's eye socket, and the eye slowly turned a smoky blue; it looked like a cracked marble. He also ended up with a permanently crinkle-cut ear. I would always go out of my way to cheer him up and show him my love, but he was never the same dog. He did not like playing second fiddle to his son. Sad. He had the softest, most beautiful coat as a young dog, and even that seemed to lose some of its lustre.

In winter 2013, I bought six in-calf black Angus heifers and was walking among them, admiring my purchases. The hounds were with me. We were about to find out one of the heifers did not abide dogs. Old one-eyed Turk did not see Number 14 coming; she blindsided him. He was tossed into the air, and she was all over him, goring him. I chased her off, and a bewildered Turk beat a hasty retreat covered in dust. To this day, Number 14 will have no truck with dogs.

Turk, Summer 2005

Number 14 minutes before rolling Turk

CHAPTER SEVEN

GRIP

Grip, Gripper, or more usually and affectionately Gripper Boy, was a biscuit coloured, black-masked, phenotypically Bull Mastiff male, despite carrying fifty percent Boerboel blood. Grip had a small fleshy knob on the top of his head, a vestigial ridge; I decided it was evidence of some Ridgeback blood in his pedigree. The largest dog of all the large dogs I have owned, Grip was a formidable and unrelenting watchdog but was otherwise a well-adjusted, very friendly and affectionate hound. He inherited none of the quirks and dodgy temperament his mother and her littermates showed.

When Grip was about seven or eight, I noticed he had grown a third testicle. Concerned with this irregularity, I showed my three-nutted dog to the vet, and Graham diagnosed it as scrotal cancer. Castration was the recommended solution. Grip had never worn a collar in his life, nor was he a bakkie dog and wasn't about to start now. The operation would have to be done at home. We placed a plastic sheet over the dining room table, and after the tranquiliser had taken effect, Graham, his assistant, and I lifted the woozy dog onto the table. He was knocked out, and the operation performed. It proved a success, and he lived into his old age with zero change of character or aggression. Grip was the only dog I ever had castrated, and that was to save his life. If only humans could bounce back from cancer as easily as dogs seem able to do.

I found the following written in July 2018:

Grip is twelve years old. He is tall and thin and walks slowly, and is often clumsy. His once black mask is grey with age, all the way back to his ears. There is a wide range of ages on the farm: Bangalory, the grey tabby cat, is fourteen years old. Taz, the Jack Russell, is thirteen. Grip twelve. Orla, the black German Shepherd, is ten, sweet but dumb as a post. Lexi, the needy Ridgeback, is six. Jango is the youngest at four: a vital, excitable, hyper-vigilant, broad muzzled, thick-coated black German Shepherd who has taken over from Grip as head of security. It is a beautiful, sunny but cool Sunday morning. Yesterday was cold and wet, so all the dogs and cat are on the front verandah enjoying the sun's rays. Jango appears immune to the cold and lies stretched out on the concrete.

And this just a month later in the log, I keep for my Angus herd:

13 August 2018 – Grip put down today, my big fella, my Big Boy Brown. Great hound. Sad day.

Grip, Winter 2011

Old man Grip, Christmas 2017

CHAPTER EIGHT

ZIGGY

Ziggy was a silky coated Great Dane x Bull Mastiff, black as night; she was gentle and refined with a noble cast to her features and would lope across the ground with great fluid bounds. When the time came for Ziggy to be spayed, she was loaded onto a bakkie with high railings. A first-time traveller, she was slightly agitated, but it was thought that the dog would soon settle down once they were on the move. Ziggy looked great in the rear-view mirror with her head up and her ears streaming in the breeze. The whites of her eyes were showing, but that was put down to the wind. By the end of the road, Ziggy had started to tap dance. Acceleration was the remedy. The bakkie barrelled into the first corner; centrifugal force would surely keep the dog glued to the floor. A quick glance backwards was just in time to see Ziggy show no regard for the laws of physics. She curled her front legs under her chest like a seasoned if suicidal showjumper and attempted to clear the railings. The vehicle came to a juddering halt with the dog hanging off the side. All hell broke loose; there was much wailing and gnashing of teeth (and that was just the owner) as he tried to push the frightened hound back onto the van. Shouts, howls, slathering growls, evacuation of bowels, and general bloodletting followed. Ziggy fled the carnage, leaving her owner pale, covered in blood and dog turd, with a hole bitten through his wrist. A scheduled vet visit ended up with an emergency trip to the doctor for stitches and a shot to negate mainlining dog poo.

A second attempt was made to get Ziggy spayed. This time a bakkie was borrowed with a reinforced canvas canopy that fitted tightly over the railings. Ziggy was heavily tranquilised under veterinary supervision – *'this will sort her out'* – then loaded woozy and apparently legless and sealed securely in the back of the vehicle. She chewed her way through the roof, popped out the top, landed lightly in the middle of the road, and cantered home before they reached the end of the drive. Peeling back her lips off a glistening set of choppers discouraged any further attempts to load her. Ziggy was eventually spayed on top of the ping pong table on the front verandah.

CHAPTER NINE

BENJ

Benj was a 65-kilogram monster of a dog, a Boerboel; he was the last survivor of a maniacal litter that included Barkly and at least two other canine psychopaths. Like the rest of his siblings, Benj was a pure nutter; by hard experience and with the scars, both physical and psychological, to prove it, his owners had learned to plan ahead for a vet visit. Dave Moberly sent me the shortlist:

1. Order double the number of sleeping tablets.

2. Convince the vet, Benj will arrive asleep.

3. Bolt the canopy on the bakkie and wire up all the windows.

4. Check the lawnmower has petrol.

5. Make sure the pre-med injection is in the fridge.

6. Check the muzzle buckles are in order and have everything needed to treat Benj on the table in the kitchen the night before.

7. Break the news gently to Elsina, the maid, and hope she will be at work the next morning.

8. Take a sleeping pill.

9. In the morning, close the entrances to the other kennels and lock the other dogs away; otherwise, all hell breaks loose.

10. Tell the children to go to their bedrooms and not watch.

11. Remind the wife she was the one who wanted the dog.

12. Feed the hound four sleeping pills – they take ages to work.

When Benj looks properly woozy, start the lawnmower. It is the critical item on the list as it is the only thing Benj fears. Benj wobbles into the kitchen retreating from the demon mower. Mom shuts the door on the dog while dad switches off the mower and begins the terrifying job of muzzling Benj.

> *"Hold the bloody head."*
>
> *"I am."*
>
> *"Not properly."*
>
> *"Just put the bloody thing on."*
>
> *"What do you think I'm doing?"*

The muzzle goes on. The pre-med next, deep, menacing growls emanate from the massive chest, plenty of swearing from dad while the rest of the family tell him how cruel he is. The pre-med is done. Thank God for that; heart rate slows down; everyone seems to quite like dad again. Elsina won't carry the end of the makeshift stretcher where Benj's head rests, she's adamant Benj will wake up, and she doesn't entirely trust the *jova*. Nor does Rasta, the vet clinic assistant;

he knows Benj's car and bolts when they arrive. Only after much coaxing and convincing will Rasta help get the sleeping lion out of the bakkie. The vet tells Dave to return in an hour; he does the job and anything else he can find that needs looking at and says this is the last time. He said that the previous three times, he's treated the dog. Benj lived into his old age, outliving all his siblings, and was much loved.

Benj

CHAPTER TEN

TIBANE & DOT

Patches, Rusty and Dot, were a litter of three brothers: fearless muscle-bound pocket rockets; they were short and stocky with broad chests and powerful jaws. Their mother was a brindle Bull Terrier; their fathers were the resident male, a Dachshund mixture and possibly a Jack Russell from across the road. Identical conformation wise, the dogs came in different colours; Patches was brown and white, Rusty was a dark brindle like his mother, and Dot was red like his sausage dog father. Two of the puppies were kept by their breeders, but the red pup moved to the Umzimkulu Valley when their son came to manage Dave Moberly's Kedron dairy herd.

Dot grew up in the calf pens, burrowing under the hay for warmth because his master neglected to provide a kennel of any sort. He lived on a diet of phutu and spilt calf milk. Extremely protective of the calves, he sorely tried the patience of Nchebe, the calf man, who he would challenge whenever he came to feed them. Dave would feel sorry for Dot, especially when it rained, and he would see the little dog sheltering all alone but for his bovine companions. Taking pity on him, Dave sorted him out with a tyre and a red lamp to keep him warm in winter.

Patches and Rusty's owners were moving and could no longer keep the dogs. They joined Dot at Kedron. The brother's reunion was not a happy one; their fights were gladiatorial. To keep the peace, Dave took Rusty. The farm staff quickly nicknamed Rusty, Tibane – Zulu for warthog – which is precisely what he looked like, with his low carriage, wide front end, slim hips, dark brindle coat and a tail that stuck straight up like an aerial. The name stuck. Patches was an iron-willed dog and quickly asserted himself as the undisputed Alpha Dog at Kedron. Hierarchy established, Dot settled into his role as follower, always with a sappy smile on his face.

Dave's manager resigned and left the district, and he gave his dogs away. As time passed, Dave started hearing stories that Patches and Dot were seen roaming in the informal settlement across the river. He decided to investigate. He found both dogs. The indefatigable Patches was thriving, the leader of a pack of five hounds. Dot was doing less well, bringing up the rear, still smiling, but the little red dog was skin and bone and covered in ticks. Dave negotiated with the new owner for the dogs. He would not give Patches up because he was such a good watchdog but let Dave take the emaciated Dot. Dave took the dog straight to the vet and had him dewormed and de-knackered before bringing him home. Sadly, Patches was killed just a week later by a neighbour who caught him eating one of his chickens.

Tibane and Dot sorted themselves out and flourished in their new home, but old habits die hard; used to surviving by their wits, they were hunters of note – if it moved, they killed and ate it. Tibane was the scourge of the garden moles, digging craters in the lawn and waiting patiently for hours to catch and gobble his prey. Dot's speciality was snakes; he has killed and consumed half a dozen night adders. Dave learned to recognize Dot's distinctive snake alarm bark and not go near the dog when he is tangling with a reptile, as Dot will not back off, and any distraction could cause him to get tagged. He has been bitten several times, his head swelling up to twice its size, and he feels very sorry for himself for a couple of days. Dave feeds him half a Disprin every morning to help with the hangover.

Tibane installed himself as the gate guard and would react with an explosion of fury if anyone dared enter the yard uninvited. Unlike Dot, who is always easy going and friendly unless provoked, Tibane was of a grumpier disposition and seriously blotted his copybook when he thrashed Zoot, the much loved, cherished and spoiled Jack Russell belonging to Dave's daughter Roxy. Despite his small size Tibane was boss of the farmyard for several years until he started having multiple uncontrollable seizures, and after he had six in one day, the sad decision was made to have him put down.

Dot had a love-hate relationship with the new dairy manager. Leon was pleased that Dot kept the genets at bay come to prey on his prized racing pigeons, but he paid a hefty price for Dot's vigilance. The dog took payment in kind and would stalk, kill and eat any pigeons that strayed beyond the electric fence installed to keep *him* out. He ate close to two dozen birds; the gamekeeper proved more costly than the poacher. Whenever Dot caught a pigeon, he would consume the whole bird leaving only the two feet with rings still attached so Leon could at least identify the deceased. Dot ever protective of his turf would tree any genets unwise enough to approach the loft. He would stake them out all night, never leaving his post. In the morning, crows would spot the poor creature and dive bomb it until it left the tree, and Dot would finish it off.

Dot has never gotten over his youthful deprivation, and he gorges on food until his belly is distended and he grunts from the discomfit. He can eat a whole cow afterbirth at a sitting. His favourite pastime is hunting sun lizards, and he is very pleased with himself when he catches a tail. Gareth, Dave's son-in-law, first introduction to Dot, was when he and Roxy went for a walk along the river with all the dogs. There was a mighty commotion in the bush, and Dot came back up the path proudly bearing a metre and a half long Legavaan in his jaws. The dog's muzzle was torn and bloody, but he had won the fight. Tough as nails, the little muscle-bound warrior has killed at least two more Legavaans. On a subsequent walk, Dot put up a rabbit, killed and ate it. Dot is not Gareth's favourite dog.

The Moberly's have long ago given up trying to call back or find Dot when he charges off into the distance after some quarry, real or imagined. If he is not back by the time they return to the bakkie, they go home and come back a few hours later, and they will find him sitting at the spot where he last saw the vehicle, waiting patiently for them to fetch him. Despite the challenges of his early life, Dot has faith in his humans. He knows they've got his back, as he has theirs.

Tibane and Dot stirring up the hounds

CHAPTER ELEVEN

FUCK OFF BUDDY

Mike Arnold reckons his oldest daughter Samantha's first spoken words were, 'Outside Jock.' Many years after the old Boerbul had departed, the Arnolds got two new puppies. Fuck Off Buddy and Fuck Off Bonny were littermates, blood-red Ridgebacks; they grew into big, good-natured dogs. Exuberantly friendly with long nut whacking tails that could fold a grown man in half, they cleared coffee tables at a single wag, trampled all over the little Jack Russell, Lady and left general carnage in their wake. They quickly earned their dubious monikers.

Bonny was magnificent, but her brother Buddy could never hold condition and was regularly plagued with maladies that left the vets scratching their heads. He was about four years old when he sickened again, and, taking a turn for the worse, the decision was made to put the dog down. Mike and Bev were away, and their foster son ended up in charge of Buddy's remains; he decided Buddy having a rough life, deserved top of the range treatment in death. He had the dog cremated and his ashes preserved in a polished wooden box; it came complete with a poem and brass plaque appropriately inscribed with his name (*sans* prefix.)

R4000 later, with poor old Fuck Off Buddy's ashes tipped out over the vegetable garden, the box now stores playing cards.

CHAPTER TWELVE

SOCKS

Socks was rescued by the SPCA. When the Colbys chose her to take home with them, she still had a raw patch around her neck where the hair had been worn away by a wire collar. A rusty yellow Labrador cross with white front paws (hence her name), she holds the record as the longest living dog the Colbys have ever owned – fifteen years. Socks was not the brightest dog, not by a long shot. She was never much of a watchdog either. Socks had one great talent, perhaps the greatest talent; she was a survivor. She was run over three times, twice by Trevor and once by Claudia, but apart from some world-class grass burns, she was none the worse for wear. A good swimmer, she escaped the flooding Vaal river, a tussle with a giant Legavaan that slapped her silly with its tail and numerous close calls with bolshy cows. But these were small achievements compared to her greatest claim to fame. Socks was the sole survivor of a mass poisoning on the farm.

Criminals intent on stealing a vehicle scattered phutu laced with Temik across the farmyard. Temik is a deadly poisonous pesticide, known locally as 'Two Step' because a dog, once ingesting it, will only take two steps before it dies. Staff arriving for morning milking were greeted by carnage; five dead dogs, dead shed cats and nearly a dozen dead chickens were scattered across the yard, and the milk delivery van pushed down the hill where it had failed to start. Socks survived by sleeping through the whole thing. Despite the mayhem outside – it was estimated the would-be car thieves were there for over an hour trying to get the vehicle started; she never left her kennel the entire night.

There is a postscript to this story; when word got out the Colbys had lost all their dogs, they were inundated with offers of replacements. Socks was quickly joined by Tyson, Foxy and Guppy. Tyson was a short-legged Boerbul with a black mask and powerful muscling; he was bow-legged and stump-tailed. Somewhere in his past, he had been badly abused as he was timid and hand shy. The sad dog seemed void of emotional displays or response until one afternoon when the Colbys were relaxing on the verandah after a long day, and he shambled over to Claudia and placed his head in her lap. On two occasions when Claudia was walking on the farm with their young sons, Tyson charged ahead and tore apart snakes about to cross their path. The silent dog proved to be a devoted bodyguard.

Socks

CHAPTER THIRTEEN

EASTWOLDS FARM

Samson and Delilah were brother and sister, purebred Bull Mastiffs with light grey coats and black masks. Great big shambling dogs, Delilah was the brains, Samson the muscle. Rob lived at the top of the hill and would drive down to dairy every morning before dawn in his Golf. The two dogs would follow him down, and when he returned home for an early breakfast, he would open the boot of the vehicle, and they would jump in for the ride back up the hill. One day he forgot to let them out when he got home. Jen hopped in the car none the wiser and drove down to Creighton, where she taught at the school. Five hours later, someone asked her why all the windows in her car were fogged up. Puzzled, Jen opened the car door, and to her horror, the melted dogs poured out onto the ground. After copious hosing down, the collapsed hounds slowly recovered and reverted to solid form, a very close call. The interior of the vehicle dripped like a tropical forest; the upholstery soaked through. Despite a thorough valeting, the dog scent never entirely left the car.

Three Jack Russells called Eastwolds home, Mozzi, Phutu and Faf, their lifespans directly correlated to their gender. Phutu uniquely batted for two innings; one winter morning, Rob heard strange sounds emanating from under the bed, knelt down to take a look and found Phutu unresponsive. The old dog had thrown a seven and croaked. Dismayed, Rob made a cup of coffee, pondering how he would break the news of the much-loved dog's demise to his family. Deciding he needed to tell the gardener to dig a hole for the dog, he got up to organise the sad task, and there on the back step was Phutu, Lazarus like, enjoying the sun with the other dogs.

Bismarck was a thick-coated black Boerboel cross. He was from the same unhinged family of dogs as Benj and Barkly; needless to say, he was a legend for all the wrong reasons.

Bismarck's rap sheet:

Exposes himself, hanging out his whanger in front of all the ladies at the wake following Rob's father's funeral.

Bites two mourners at the same wake. In Bismarck's defence, one of the victims, three sheets to the wind, tried to tackle the dog.

Bites Rob's nephew's mother-in-law.

Chews up one of the small dogs, requiring an emergency vet visit.

Bites Rob's daughter when she trips over him lying in the doorway. Rob contests this; Emily points out he drew blood.

Bites Rob's brother-in-law.

Bites a local commissioner of oaths.

Bites a sales rep, who phoned the next day to politely inquire if Bismarck's rabies vaccinations were up to date.

Bites one of the waitresses at a fine dining lunch held at Eastwolds.

Chews up another small dog, requiring another vet visit.

When visiting Eastwolds, I would wait in my vehicle for a friendly face to appear and escort me into the safety of the house while the delinquent hound circled my bakkie barking and growling. Rob was very attached to Bismarck and cheerfully glossed over his many transgressions, arguing he only bit when provoked, stepped on or bumped into. Still, I can't say I missed the grumpy old bugger when he overheated and expired, accompanying Jen on her farm walk – the activity he enjoyed most when he wasn't biting people.

CHAPTER FOURTEEN

ORLA

I have always preferred Mastiff type dogs, with their big black-masked heads and short, broad muzzles, but I have owned four German Shepherds: Joad, Orla, Georgia, and Jango. At one time, much to my surprise, I owned three sharp-nosed dogs at once. Joad was my first, the aforementioned one-eighth wolf who was given such a hard time by Strike. He came into his own after Strike died, Joad and Skyler were good friends, and Turk never bothered him.

Orla was my second Shepherd. I had been looking for a German Shepherd of a specific type for a long time: a wide front-ended, strong-boned animal. Friends of mine were looking for a similar type of dog, and we thought we had hit the jackpot when we found an advert for puppies described as being from British police dog stock; the photo showed a sturdy, broad-backed dog standing squarely on its four legs. We drove up to Pretoria to fetch our pups. R7000 was the most I had ever paid for a dog, and I never told anybody for a long time. Ed chose a black and tan female, and I took the pure black female. Orla was a delightful pup and looked like a woolly bear cub. She grew into a thick-coated medium-sized dog who rarely barked, even when the other dogs sounded off in full alarm mode. She would often give a few yaps five minutes after all was quiet, with the rest of the pack already returned to their beds.

My dogs are pets, but they also have a job to do; they must keep me safe and are an integral part of my security system. Orla scored 100 as a pet and zero at the other thing. She would have enjoyed a happy, uneventful life but for the fateful arrival of her littermate. Georgia's owners were moving and could not take all their many dogs and at least a dozen cats with them. They asked me if I would like to take Georgia. I happily agreed. Mistake. Georgia was a stunningly beautiful dog and well trained to boot. Unfortunately, it was not a happy reunion. Georgia and Orla hated each other, and Georgia proved to be a serial cat killer.

6 May 2019 – Gareth put Orla down. She had lost a lot of weight over the last couple of months until she was almost skin and bone. He said she had a big tumour on her liver. She slept next to my bed last night. Useless watchdog, but hugely affectionate pet; she would cry with joy whenever I arrived home. Good girl.

Orla

Georgia, Orla, Jango and Grip

CHAPTER FIFTEEN

JANGO

Jango is a delight. He is a big black German Shepherd dog with a thick coat. Seven years old at the time of writing, he is the alpha dog on the farm. He is hyper-vigilant and an excellent watchdog. He was born on the van Deventer's back verandah and reared there as a pup. He is the only dog I have ever owned that required zero toilet training; I put it down to the fact he always had access to the lawn as a young pup. Having a dog that has never crapped or peed in the house ranks high on my reasons to be cheerful list.

Jango's parents were Jess and Jet. Jess was an expensive purchase, supposedly a pure German Shepherd, but she never grew bigger than and looked like a shaggy border collie. What she lacked in size, she made up in alertness, a great little guard dog, she had an iron will and reigned supreme over the other dogs on the property, a real matriarch. Jet is a pitch-black, smooth-coated, slimly built German Shepherd. As laid back as his mate was hardcore, his favourite pastime is chasing birds. Genes will out; Jango inherited his mother's thick coat and the bird chasing obsession from his father; he continually stalks and flushes any Hadedahs that dare land on the lawn. He will chase pigeons and stare and bark up at them when they perch on the power lines. Very occasionally, he catches one.

Jango is rude when it comes to demanding affection. Skyler and Grip would gently lay their muzzles on my leg for a pat when I was working at my desk. Not Jango; he pokes you under the arm – hard and without invitation – and keeps poking until he gets an appropriate response. I give him (sometimes grumpy) robust pats on the head or a hug, and he settles down for a nap. His favourite spot to sleep is the gap between my desk and the recliner. Occasionally he will lie on the couch, but never for very long. The slightest noise triggers him to explode from the house, baying blue murder. A passionate night time howler, especially if the jackals are noisy, he will whip the other dogs into a frenzy of mournful howling. Car and fence alarms have a similar effect on him.

He loves accompanying me when I inspect my Angus cows. He knows Number 14 and gives all the cows a wide berth and tracks far and wide over the veld, following his nose. One shout of 'come dogs,' from me, and he heads back home obediently.

Jango

CHAPTER SIXTEEN

JACK RUSSELLS

There are two species of Jack Russell; male and female. A word to the tender of heart, never own a Jack Russell male. They have such short shelf lives they should be sold in six-packs at the local co-op. They are the cannon fodder of the canine world. Careless with their lives, they are fearless to the point of extinction. They throw themselves down holes, into the jaws of Rottweilers, and in front of cars with such reckless zeal, it is frankly amazing the breed exists. The evolutionary glitch with Jack Russell males is that their ball to body mass ratio is out of whack; the testosterone overload clouds their judgement. It makes them think they are bigger, faster, and stronger than all other dogs. That they kill themselves with such cheerful enthusiasm is testimony to the fact there are more than a few loose connections in their wiring.

Captain, is a case in point; he was hardly out of puppyhood when he had his first close encounter of the vehicular kind, trying to stop a Toyota bakkie by jumping under the front wheel. Only a mad rush to the vet and some fancy needlework to fix the hole in his diaphragm saved his life. A R300 dog was suddenly a R3000 investment. He was back hunting bakkies in a month. His next target was my Isuzu; I crawled down the drive and only accelerated when I was quite sure he was gone; there was a bump followed by a sound not unlike the ringing of the cash register in the veterinary clinic as he ran home. Captain had a black stripe from ear to tail courtesy of my rear tyre. He returned from the vets bent out of shape – literally; he was curved like a banana and walked around crab-like for a couple of weeks. He eventually straightened out, but from then on, he barked rudely and incessantly at me whenever I visited his owners.

Jack Russells and big dogs are a grave mixture. Captain persecuted Buster, the new Boerboel pup, mercilessly. Buster got his own back when he grew up. He was found tossing and catching Captain in the air like a killer whale playing with a seal. Jack Russells do not know the meaning of retreat; each time Captain came to earth, he would charge back ferociously for more. Curiously attached to Captain and eager to protect their growing investment in the dog, the Boerboel's teeth were filed down. Buster became a very frustrated dog.

Captain's next stunt was worthy of Indiana Jones. He was on the back of the bakkie loaded with fertiliser bags, having a barking match with Buster running alongside the vehicle. When Buster overtook the bakkie, Captain could not contain himself. He scrambled onto the roof, slid down the windscreen, charged across the bonnet, and leapt off the front end, disappearing under the vehicle. He re-appeared in the rearview mirror, tumbling end over end; he was dusty and dishevelled but otherwise unhurt. True to the psychopathy of these dogs, Captain learnt nothing from these near-death experiences and subsequently bounced off the wheel of a Toyota Hilux at 70 kilometres an hour. He made a dying cockroach impression for ten minutes, all four legs in the air, then stood up and wobbled stiffly home. Sadly, a vehicle did finally do him in.

I have been lucky enough to own two legendary Jack Russells. Jos was my first; her mother Candy pretended to be a refined lap dog, but like all Jack Russells, she was a stone killer and once chased a porcupine so deep down an ant bear hole she had to be dug out with the blade of a Ford County tractor. She emerged with a quill in her butt and another in her neck. Candy loved nothing better than to be let out of the bakkie and run ahead of the vehicle through the cane fields. You had to watch her carefully as she would always run a couple of hundred yards and then suddenly stop and take a crap before charging off again.

Jos' father, Squiggles, was a small, rough-coated dog of mixed breed. He arrived on the farm with a chewed off cord around his neck; he disappeared as suddenly as he had appeared, only to return a few days later with an even thicker chewed off rope around his neck and never left. Disagreeable – human calves just above the top of a gumboot were his favourite snack; he had chronic halitosis, and his farts could drop birds out the sky. Built like a furry brick, he was run over so many times he seemed to be doing it on purpose until it was realised he was hard of hearing. I glanced in the rear-view mirror one day and saw him challenge my chasing bull mastiff. Tarn picked him up on the bounce, shook him a couple of times, and tossed him into the hydrangeas, all without breaking his stride.

Squiggles survived forty-eight hours locked in a cold room; he was found curled in a ball, with his nose plugged firmly under his tail, no doubt keeping warm by inhaling his nuclear emissions. Despite all odds, Squiggles lived into old age, growing deafer and smellier until he took a fateful nap behind the tyre of a parked vehicle. The old boy never heard the car starting.

Jos was a faithful companion for fourteen years. Brave, she took on her first rat when she was just a pup, barely outweighing the big male she cornered on the back verandah. I eventually had to step in when it looked like the rat was getting the upper hand. Despite this inauspicious start, she became a ratter of note. She was just a tiny pup when I took her on a walk to the main irrigation dam and back. At one point, I had to jump over a narrow spillway gushing water. Jos did not hesitate, and as small as she was, she leapt into the water and swam across to join me. She loved retrieving sticks of any size thrown into water, even in the surf. She once disappeared into the reeds after a thrown stick and emerged with a Spurwing gosling in her jaws. I also caught her crossing the farmyard, head held high with a kitten in her mouth. I rescued the cat and returned it to its mother.

Jos loved being a farm manager's dog and hated my career change when I joined a genetics company selling bull semen to dairy farmers, and she had to stay home. I could always rely on her to be waiting at the gate on my return. When I did army camps, Bo would take her with him in the front of his bakkie; otherwise, she would sit at my gate all day watching the road, standing up every time a vehicle approached in the forlorn hope it was me returning home. That puts a lump in my throat even now.

Jos

As she grew older, Jos became more and more anxious when a storm was brewing. She would crawl into my lap and shiver while thunder and lightning crashed outside. The day she disappeared, there had been a terrific storm in the afternoon. I think she was making her way to my neighbours (she had done this before), and her heart gave out. I hope that is what happened. I searched the road in case she had been run over but never found a body, and she would never have got into a stranger's car. Fantastic dog.

Rizzo was my next Jack Russell. A little cracker, she was just coming into her own at two years of age when she was killed by Barkly, and Red got his trophy wife.

Rizzo

Then came Taz. Another legendary Jack Russell. She was about three years old when I went to visit my sister June in Durban. I always took Taz with me. Taz sickened over the weekend, and by the Monday morning, when I should have been heading home, she was extremely ill. We took her to the local vet. It took her some weeks to recover, and with June grown so attached to her, she ended up staying in Durban. Taz had two great canine companions in her life, Jess and Lexi. June had lost her husband some years before, and soon after Gerald died, I bought her a Boerboel cross she named Jess. Jess was a beautiful puppy that grew into an ugly dog. Tall and narrow with a deep chest, she had bad legs and was very ungainly with weird helicopter blade ears. I saw both her parents, and they were beautiful dogs, but poor old Jess ended up on the wrong end of the bell curve genetically. Fortunately, her size put the fear of God into people, and June loved her. Jess and Taz became tremendous pals, and Taz would always sleep on top of her. When June sold her house and purchased a new home, she had to stay in a flat for a couple of months before taking occupation; Jess and Taz came to live with me for that period.

Jess was fascinated by the cats and would follow Bangalory everywhere, her nose always just a step or two behind her. Bangalory was in no danger; the older Jess got, the more ungainly the dog had become, and she could never quite catch up to her. I'm not sure what her intentions were had she ever caught up to the cat.

When Jess died, I replaced her with Lexi, a Ridgeback I sourced in Estcourt. Lexi grew into a magnificent specimen of her breed. She was an excellent watchdog with a booming blood-curdling bark. The ideal dog for two women living independently, June shared the house

Jess stalking Bangalory

with her best friend, Marlene. The merry widows I called them. Taz and Lexi became firm friends. They were spoiled rotten by June and Marlene and always had special treats. Taz idolised June and rarely let her out of her sight. June worked from home. Taz would lie in her basket next to her desk; if June went to the kitchen or the loo, Taz would follow her there. My sister died in March 2017 after a two-year battle with pancreatic cancer. Taz slept on June's bed on the last night of her life. She did not move from her side until the undertakers took away her body.

After June died, Taz and Lexi came to live with me. I had high expectations of Lexi. She had been such a tremendous watchdog for

June and Marlene. It was not to be; Lexi battled to adapt to her new circumstances. She was used to being queen of all she surveyed; as innocuous a dog as Orla was, she completely dominated the young Ridgeback. Fortunately, Lexi and Jango, my German Shepherd, got on well. When Lexi farts, she always jumps up in surprise as though it wasn't her that made the sound. I think she learned that from my sister. Lexi is nine years old now; she recently went in for a service and had all her lumps and bumps removed. She looks like a new dog.

Twelve-year-old Taz was unfazed by the move; she had lived here before – twice. Taz ignored the other dogs and everything else she was not immediately busy with. She was totally fearless and would walk between the Angus heifers; if they came too close, she would show them a curled lip or give them a quick snap and carry on about her business. She was always busy, always bustling, always hunting and exploring, her sharp inquiring nose in the grass or a crack in the concrete. She had a way of plopping down on her bum and intently watching you with wise old eyes.

Taz had got too old and stiff to jump onto my bed, I placed an old pouffe next to the bed, and she would jump onto it first and then onto the bed, but more often than not, she needed my hand under her backside to help her up. She would sit next to me on the bed and nudge me with her paw until I gave her a rub and a pat. As old and threadbare as she was, I used to tell Taz I needed her to live a long time. And then the most terrible thing happened:

18 August 2019 – I rode over and killed Taz today. Grief, grief, grief. My little Tazneem who slept on my bed every night. Constant companion and loyal, loyal dog, I loved her so. She was born on the 6th of January 2005 and had a good life here and for ten years with June in Durban.

Her collar sits on a shelf of my bookcase still.

Lexi and Taz

CHAPTER SEVENTEEN

FOX CREEK CRUISER

I came to know Cruiser when Henk Coetsee was the manager at Sarsgrove Farm in Mooi River. I would visit once a month and make bull recommendations for all the cows that had calved in the previous thirty days. This would take all afternoon, and I would often stay overnight at Henk and Adele Coetsee's home; dog lovers, they owned a black and tan Bull Terrier with floppy ears, a Miniature Pinscher called Basjan and three rough-coated Jack Russell terriers. Two females and Cruiser, a friendly older male with one blue eye, who was as calm as the girls were hyper.

Cruiser's sire was an imported dog called Beckett who had won all the prizes in the South African Jack Russell Club and had been Stud Dog of the year multiple times. Cruiser's dam, Caz, a very well-bred dog in her own right, gave birth to four pups, two males and two females. Three of the puppies were feisty, Cruiser was laid back and calm, he was always the last to learn new things, but Henk was impressed with how he was put together, he had the build Henk was looking for – thick legs, nice head, strong neck, straight back. Henk kept two puppies, one of the females and the quiet, self-contained male he registered as Fox Creek Cruiser. He was puzzled when he received the dog's papers back to find the pup had been registered as Fox Creek Cuthbert. Many pedigree dog breeders like to extend their authority over their dog's progeny even after selling the pups with all manner of caveats as to how they can and cannot be bred, etcetera. Caz's breeder had unilaterally decided Cuthbert was a better name than Cruiser. Henk very quickly got the name rectified, and Cruiser he remained.

Caz, Phoebe (Cruiser's littermate), Cruiser and Cider

Jack Russell's were bred to hunt; all my Jack Russells have been superb ratters. Cruiser was two years old when Henk started working him, hunting jackals. He had already caught and killed a couple of mongooses taking shortcuts through their garden. Cruiser was not an aggressive dog; whenever there were dog fights, he would not enter the fray, he did not hide, he just did not fight and would stand apart and watch – hunting was his thing, not fighting.

One Christmas eve, with all the family visiting, Henk and his brother and his brother's girlfriend took the dogs for a run in the late afternoon – four Jack Russells and a young Greyhound. The dogs were enjoying themselves, coursing across the veld when a jackal popped out of the knee-high eragrostis grass directly in front of them. The five dogs took off after it. They watched the jackal cross the valley and climb the hill on the far side with the Greyhound nipping at its heels and about to catch it when it disappeared down a hole. All four Jack Russells disappeared down the hole after it. The sun was setting, and storm clouds were gathering when they managed to call three of the four Jack Russells out the tunnel. Cruiser was not one of them. They would have to dig him out.

By the time they returned home, it was raining a monsoon. A very unhappy Adele told Henk to "go back and get that dog tonight." Henk and his brother, armed with a pick and shovel, dug in the rain by torchlight until midnight to no avail. Henk knew that UK breeders would leave a jacket next to the hole that contained a lost dog, and invariably the dog would be found lying on his master's jacket come morning. Henk left his coat next to the tunnel. He returned first thing in the morning; his sodden jacket was still there – but no dog or any sound from him. Later that morning, Henk fetched the farm's TLB (Tractor-Loader-Backhoe), a machine he had never operated before. He quickly acquainted himself with the controls, and with his brother shining a torch down the hole and shouting instructions, he started digging trenches every three or four meters in search of the terrier. At any moment, they expected to find a drowned dog, and there was always the danger that Henk could cut the dog in two with the trenching blade. They followed the twist and turns of the underground tunnel for a hundred meters with no sign of Cruiser.

This all took time; Christmas lunch was looming, the missed calls were piling up on their phones, and when they did answer, the brothers were threatened with their lives if they were late for lunch, in addition to the suggested loss of life if they returned without the dog. They were in danger of being killed twice on Christmas day.

Henk's subsequent excavation revealed an underground waterfall, a one-and-a-half-meter vertical bend in the tunnel. They found Cruiser at the bottom of the waterfall, unable to jump back up; he was wet and cold and covered in mud and sitting on top of the dead jackal. Henk's brother went to grab him and was nearly bitten for his troubles. Cruiser was exhausted but still very protective of his kill. It was now twelve o clock. They quickly locked the dog in the bakkie canopy, repaired all their excavations and returned the very slow-moving TLB to its garage before going home. They arrived back just as everyone was dishing up for lunch. They were the same colour mud as Cruiser but quickly hosed themselves off and joined the family. Hostile looks greeted them at the table, barely mollified by the dog's safe return, and they were not popular for many days afterwards. Cruiser was none the worse for wear and would go on to notch up thirty-six solo jackal kills in his lifetime.

Cruiser's first dog show was not a success; he was asked to leave the ring. When Henk asked the judge, what was wrong with the dog, he was given a list of the dogs' many faults and told his terrier did not fit what the breed wanted. Undeterred Henk entered him in the Freestate regional champs; Cruiser didn't win but wasn't kicked out of the ring either and placed third or fourth. His next show was a three-way-meet, held on a farm near Harrismith. To avoid any accusations of bias, this show had an international judge, a Welshman. Cruiser and another dog were the last two dogs left in the competition. The judge could not make up his mind between the dogs; they were so evenly matched. A bird high in a gumtree gave an alarm call; Cruiser reacted immediately and snapped into full alert mode, his head cocked and his ears up. The other dog did not respond. Cruiser was made Supreme Champion of the show. Cruiser became a legend in the South African Jack Russell breed: he was Stud Dog of the Year for several years in a row. He also won the coveted Working Terrier of the Year gold medallion several times. He sired multiple litters of pups and significantly impacted the pedigrees of registered Jack Russell dogs in this country.

The practice after shows was to take the judge hunting; these were working dogs after all. Henk was nominated to organize the hunt after his success at the three-way-meet. The Kamberg valley where

Henk worked was overrun with jackals. There was one particularly wily animal that would go to ground in burrows that contained a porcupine. Porcupines enter holes head first, so any chasing predator gets a face full of quills. This smart jackal would squeeze past the porcupine and sit face to face behind it, hiding from the dogs. A junior member of the club at that time, Henk left Cruiser locked up in his box while other more experienced breeders sent in their dogs after the jackal, all were unsuccessful and returned bristling with quills. The Welsh judge said, "Bring me that supreme champion." Cruiser needed no second bidding; he was going ballistic in his cage, trying to chew through mesh and wood to join the hunt. He went down the hole, got past the porcupine unscathed, found and killed the jackal. Another clever jackal would dart from den to den, confusing the dogs by trailing its scent through the maze of tunnels while it hid in a side shaft. Cruiser got him too.

Cruiser had two faults, he hated being locked up in his cage at shows or hunts and would destroy any box Henk constructed, chewing his way through wood and expanded mesh to get out, ruining his teeth in the process. He would also express his disgust at being caged by peeing in his water bowl.

Cruiser dealt with snakes the same way he dealt with jackals. Henk visited the family farm in Aliwal North and had two Jack Russell's with him, a female named Cider and Cruiser. Cider cornered a large male dassie and came off second best. Dassies are formidable quarry, and Cider found out the hard way that they have a sharp end when it bit her on the tongue and would not let go. Hearing her screams, Henk rushed to her aid but was beaten by Cruiser, who gave the dassie short shrift. One morning they drove into town, leaving the two dogs in the fenced-in backyard. When they returned home a few hours later, they found both the dogs covered in blood. They had killed a one-and-a-half-meter long Cape Cobra – the hapless snake lay in two-inch pieces strewn about the yard. Sure, they would have been tagged by the deadly snake; Henk carefully held each dog under a hosepipe, combing through the wet fur looking for the tell-tale double puncture wound, and was mightily relieved when he found none.

Cruiser killed his last snake, a Rinkhals, when he was in his dotage. Adele heard their dogs sounding the alarm, barking and yapping excitedly at the back door. She found the cornered spitting cobra's hood spread wide in defiance, the baying hounds wisely keeping their distance. She phoned Henk to come and help. By the time Henk got home, the old boy, nearly deaf and blind in one eye with teeth worn to stumps, roused from his nap by the commotion, had already dispatched the snake. Henk gave Cruiser the water treatment again, but he had killed the snake without it biting him.

In all his jackal hunting years and many brushes with porcupines, Cruiser never lost an eye. He was a pensioner living the good life in Mooi River when it happened. It was a very dry year, and in the drought conditions, rabbits, porcupines and even a wild pig came into the Coetzee's garden looking for food. The dogs cornered a porcupine. When Henk came home, Tux, the bull terrier, had a face full of quills. Cruiser was unscathed but for a pinprick of blood in his left eye. Slowly over time, the eye turned blue, and he lost his sight in it.

Cruiser reached the grand old age of sixteen, and the time had come to put him down. Toothless, blind and deaf, he sometimes fell into such a deep sleep that when picked up, he was more ragdoll than dog; many times, he was thought to be dead only to stir after vigorous shaking. Henk would soften his pellets with warm water to make a gruel that the dog could eat. Every morning he would be put on the lawn to do his business and then placed back in his box where he would sleep away the day, only very occasionally venturing out on his own. Andy, the vet, came every Wednesday for weekly herd runs, but Henk kept putting off the inevitable. A change of jobs forced his hand; Cruiser knew his current home but would be unfamiliar with new surroundings, it would not be fair to take the old dog to strange places. Finally, it was the last Wednesday before Henk was leaving:

"That morning I dug the hole myself, then after the vet visit Andy parked his bakkie at the calves, and I told him I was going to fetch the dog . . . and you know how kak that is, to go and fetch the dog . . . you are going to kill the bloody thing . . . but you are also relieving the pain and suffering. I mean, sometimes he is fast asleep, and he pisses himself. He was old, sixteen and he hadn't lived on the couch, he had worked, killed jackals . . . So, I took him there and gave him to Andy, and I walked into the calves, and I gave him a black bag because I didn't want to see. When it was done, I just greeted Andy and got in my bakkie and drove home and buried him. And when I buried that dog, I cried."

Old man Cruiser with Ora.

CHAPTER EIGHTEEN

KIRKMAN CRESCENT

Hobo was our first family dog. He was a Doberman x Alsatian, black and tan, with a rough coat and a docked tail. We were living in Johannesburg when my father bought Hobo from a local pet shop. Dad was a Railwayman and would take promotion wherever it took him. Hobo came with us when we moved to Kimberly a few years later, and I started school. Hobo loved kippers and would drool at the kitchen door when they were on the menu. He also liked to patrol the neighbourhood and would jump over the front gate to explore. You always knew when he left or returned because his backfoot clipped the top of the gate, and the chain would rattle. When my old man got a promotion to the Durban office, we moved into a flat in Currie Road near the Greyville Racecourse. Hobo could not come with us, and he was put in a crate and sent by train to my uncle's farm in Ixopo. He enjoyed the farm but was always very happy to see us when we visited.

After the flat, we moved into one of four brand new Railway houses built on Kirkman Crescent on the Bluff. Five very different dogs coloured our Bluff years, only one of which was ours. Sabre was of undetermined breed, a medium-sized, good looking dog. He had a thick red coat with a golden mane, feathered legs and a feathered tail that curled over his back. Dad loved to flea him and, in the evenings after he had read the newspapers, he would put the dog on the table and pop any fleas he found by snapping them under his thumbnail. Sabre would submit to these long grooming sessions without resistance.

Dutchie was a Dachshund from two houses down who would charge over to our place in the afternoons when we got home from school. Sabre and Dutchie were great mates. The little Daksie was neglected, her owners giving her very sporadic attention, and my father took to giving her a saucer of food when he got home after work. Loyal as the day is long, she would always return to her own home in the evenings. One day she didn't turn up, and we never saw her again. There were horrible rumours as to what had become of her, but they were never confirmed.

Woofy was Sabre's next playmate. She was also from two houses down but in the opposite direction. Another pavement special, Woofy, was sturdily built, with short legs, a long body and a tail like an antenna over her back. A constant presence at our house, she was a very successful mole hunter and would stalk her prey for hours, her head cocked, listening for movement in their underground tunnels.

Then there was Butch. He lived four houses down and belonged to friends of ours, the Mansers. Butch was scary; if he ever got out the yard, we shat ourselves and scattered. He was mostly Boxer but built with all the power and malevolence of a Jaguar. He got hold of Sabre one day and was giving him a proper mauling. Sabre was in mortal danger; we screamed and shouted at Butch to stop but were too scared to get close. All our protestations and feeble attempts at stopping him were to no avail. Sabre was going to die. Darryl Manser snapped off a branch from a nearby tree and, stripping it of leaves, stuck it up Butch's behind. The surprised dog let Sabre go.

Wagter belonged to an Afrikaans family that lived next door to the Mansers. A rangy Boerbul, he lived permanently chained to a long wire stretched across the backyard. He and Butch would have jaw frothing barking matches through the fence. When *Wagter* got too old, they took off his collar and phoned the cops and told them there was a mad dog in their yard that needed removing. Heartless.

I remember one other dog incident from the Bluff, a Keeshond who lived at the top of the road, charged out the gate and bit my sister Mary on the back when she was learning to ride a bicycle.

I was in the army when I received a letter from my father telling me Sabre had died. He was twelve years old; he had come to us when I was in junior school, a much loved and loving family pet. That evening I sat on top of the earthen revetment wall encircling the base and dedicated our daily ration of two beers to the old boy. I probably shed a tear.

Sabre

CHAPTER NINETEEN

CATS

I like cats. I have three of them; Cisco is the best one – that's what I tell him when he jumps on the bed in the morning for a scratch and a cuddle. Growing up in Durban, we would visit our maternal grandmother and uncle on their farm in Ixopo several times a year and every Christmas while Gran was still alive. There were always kittens to play with, cranked out by the same small grey cat that seemed to live permanently on Gran's bed. Not particularly friendly (the cat, I mean, Gran was great), she was there forever and probably reared a hundred kittens in her lifetime.

Visits to Carisbrooke were the highlights of my childhood. I loved the farm: eating *phutu* dry just with sugar and no milk, flapjacks and the best roast potatoes in the world (my mother's tended to be armour-plated), watching my uncle stick his false eye back in its socket every morning, he kept it in a small water-filled enamel basin on the chest of drawers overnight. I remember crapping myself when a large frog jumped out of an old rain-filled tyre and landed on my chest and becoming somewhat distraught when Jane, the spayed mastiff x ridgeback, vigorously humped my leg when I was about ten or eleven.

Back home on the Bluff, we had a hefty black and white cat called Hague. He was an easy-going, slow-moving, bow-legged cat who didn't do much of anything besides eating and sleeping and occasionally leave the property for what we regarded as a harmless tour of the neighbourhood. This proved to be a bad idea: one morning, my father found him lying dead in an open space between the houses. Hague had been shot. Many of our neighbours kept pigeons. Perhaps the cat was spotted near a loft, but he was so well fed and seriously unathletic; I doubt he was ever a threat. Owner's bias, I know, but I cannot understand that sort of cruelty.

When my father retired, my folks moved to Hillary. One morning dad found a young tortoiseshell cat hiding in the garage. She was starving, so he started putting out food for her. She slowly overcame her fear and eventually moved into the house. He named her Purdy after the Joanna Lumley character in the New Avengers television series. Purdy was pregnant and delivered two kittens in the bottom of my mother's wardrobe. We persuaded the folks to keep both kittens, and the ginger tom was inevitably named Gambit. I named the little female Havoc after one of the wild dogs featured in the book Innocent Killers by Hugo van Lawick and Jane Goodall. It proved a very apt name. Gambit was only two or three years old when he was hit by a car, but Purdy and Havoc lived to a good age.

I had a couple of cats when I was farm managing. One was a little tabby female whose name I cannot remember, nor can I recall what happened to her. She was more dog than cat and would follow me everywhere, getting sopping wet when walking through the pastures.

I do know I hitchhiked down to Durban to visit my folks, with her tucked inside my shirt when she was a kitten. It was before the toll road was built, and I was waiting for a lift on the old Durban road after being dropped off at the Hillcrest turnoff, and she peed all over me. I never explained my wet shirt or any possible odour or revealed that I had a cat hidden on my person when I got my next ride.

Korkina was a feral cat we found abandoned in the undergrowth as a tiny kitten. It was January 2001, and I was working on my smallholding with my then herdsman, and I heard a kitten mewing. I asked him if he could hear it – he said no. We looked for the kitten but could not find it. I had to go but told him there was definitely a kitten there, and when he found it, he should bring it up to the house. When I arrived home that evening, a tiny kitten was waiting for me in a cardboard box. A very hungry and noisy kitten that required bottle feeding. I named her Korkina after the beautiful and supple Russian Olympic gymnast Svetlana Khorkina. Korkina, like her namesake, was a very lithe and acrobatic cat. She would leave the fenced-in homestead and hunt in the bush all day, but when she heard my Isuzu coming up the drive, she would return home. I would often see her coursing across the Kikuyu grass, coming to meet me. By the time I got into the house, she would be there. A hunter of note, she was also very affectionate. Her favourite spot was my lap whenever I was docked for the night on my recliner, either watching television or asleep, two of my Olympic level pastimes.

My dogs always get excited when I get home, the Alsatians especially. Ninety-nine per cent of dog fights are precipitated by over-excited dogs turning on each other when I come up the drive, so I usually debus as quickly as possible and shit on everybody and yell at them to shut up and get out of the bloody way. It is a joyous occasion for all. Even more so, if the gate motor is on the blink, and I have to get out and open the gate manually.

Korkina, the orphan kitten

I got home early one afternoon in February 2012 and, for once, didn't get out of the car immediately because I was enjoying the song playing on the radio. I think it was Black Sabbath. When I eventually walked onto the verandah, I saw Korkina lying dead in the corner. Mortified, I scooped her up. She was stiff but still warm, and I could see she was breathing. She appeared to be paralysed or in a coma. My immediate thoughts were she had been poisoned or bitten by a snake. I called the new young vet, and we met on the side of the road. Jackie could not diagnose the problem but gave Korkina an injection or two and told me I needed to take her through to the surgery in Howick.

Korkina did not stir the entire trip, and when I lifted her out of the vehicle, she was still as stiff as a board. The receiving vet examined the cat but could not find a reason for her paralysed state, she was put on a drip, and we hoped for the best. Korkina lay like that for three days. On the fourth day, she started lifting her head whenever they looked in on her, and after a week, she could just about sit up and fall over again. Stumped as to what ailed her and determined to find the cause, one of the vets examined the cat minutely and finally found a tiny puncture wound in the top of her skull. Probably from a canine tooth. Probably an opportunistic snap from an over-excited hound while the boss sat in his car listening to music.

I would visit Korkina once a week, and she would purr away when I held her. Tear inducing stuff. I think she was at the clinic for just shy of a month, she was improving ever so slowly, and there was not much more they could do for my brain-injured moggy, so I brought 2012's most expensive cat home. Overnight Korkina went from lithe gymnast to wobbly cat. It was fascinating to watch her recovery; she never fully regained her balance and, for the rest of her life, had a funny elongated gait. She would still try and jump onto tables and window sills, and there would be a mighty crash when she missed or fell off. Georgia was not yet at New Leaf, and I always suspect Grip had bitten Kork.

Korkina

It wasn't Korkina's first time at the vet. I came home one day to find her with a broken back leg, cause unknown. A quick trip to the vet and her leg was set in plaster. I shut her in the back room with food and water and a litter box. I don't think the cast stayed on her leg for more than a couple of days. Despite this, the leg mended quickly with just a little bump on the bone where it had snapped. Andy Lund, a very experienced local vet, jokes that cats and their broken bones only have to be in the same room to heal. I found Korkina lying dead in the backyard about a year after her brain injury. She was twelve years old. In hindsight, I am sure Georgia killed her.

Bangalory was a shed cat from a dairy farm in Nottingham Road. I was admiring the beautiful kittens, and the owners asked if I wanted one. I happily said yes. I put the kitten in the cab with me, not bothering with a box – bad move – the ninety-minute trip home was a nightmare; the terrified moggy caromed around the interior of the cab, bouncing off doors, windows and roof like a furry bullet. When she wasn't airborne, she crawled all over me or hid under the seat or wedged herself between the dashboard and windscreen, meowing piteously. Even more hair raising was when she ended up under the foot pedals a couple of times. I would try and hold her and keep her calm, and was scratched and bitten for my troubles.

As much as Bangalory tried to make friends with Korkina, Kork was not interested and would repulse her overtures with lightning strikes of her paw. They eventually developed a relationship of sorts; it was more ceasefire than peace. Bangalory was eight and Korkina eleven when Georgia arrived. The cats realised before me that her interest in them was deadly rather than friendly. If her previous owners had warned me (they must have known), I would never have taken her. I did notice both cats were using a back window if they needed to go outside. They would only venture out the front if I was home. They knew Georgia was not to be trusted.

I was visiting a Franklin dairy some months after Korkina died and was offered two playful kittens, a little ginger tom with a white chest and his pitch-black sister. I said I would take the kittens and, having learnt my lesson transported them home in a sturdy cardboard box. I named them Jinx and Tombi. Bangalory greeted them with about the same degree of enthusiasm Korkina had welcomed her arrival. They quickly crept into my heart, and I loved to watch their skylarking. At this point, I had not fully realised I had introduced a cat killer into the homestead. Six weeks later, in July of that year, I travelled to America to look at cows – specifically the progeny of the bulls we sell. I was away for two weeks and returned to a household with all animals present and correct and happy to see me.

Home a week, I fell asleep watching highlights of the London Summer Olympics with both the kittens snuggled on my person. I woke up in the night, and only Jinx was there. I woke again; Tombi was still not back. The kittens had survived a fortnight on their own when I was in the USA, but that night when Tombi went outside to do her business, Georgia got her. I found her tiny, mauled body on the front lawn the next morning. Fucking dog.

Some days later, I was watching more of the Olympics with Jinx sitting on my lap. I got excited when Usain Bolt smoked the competition, and the startled kitten jumped off my lap. I thought nothing of it, but Jinx must have gone outside, and Georgia, possibly alerted by my cheers, snaffled him. Fucking, fucking dog.

I did not mourn Georgia when she died. She was buried in a quiet corner of a Kikuyu pasture. You don't get a spot in the garden if you kill my cats. A week after the dog was gone, I found Bangalory sunning herself on the front verandah. She had not done that in a very long time.

Bangalory could obviously play the long game; she survived Georgia's predations and endured Korkina's reign. Korkina and Bangalory were never great mates, and though they would occasionally sit together, it often ended in a scuffle.

Korkina and Bangalory

Korkina commanded my lap. When Korkina died, Bangalory became a different cat overnight. After eight years of pretty much ignoring me, she became an affectionate pet and my best buddy. She shared my bed for the rest of her days and loved sleeping on my lap. She was a profound sleeper and would relax into an almost liquid state across my knees.

Bangalory had a good innings; she had been an excellent ratter in her youth, bringing home some monsters. I would crank up the volume on the television when she ate them, as listening to a cat crunching through her kill is not one of the world's most invigorating sounds. Always in good nick with a beautiful coat, Bango got progressively thinner in her last months. She was ailing, and I took her to the vet. My options were, have her put down, or they could perform a procedure that would give her some relief. I stupidly, sentimentally said, let's try the op. Bangalory's last three weeks were terrible. She spent most of the time lying on my bed, and when she disappeared, I thought she had gone off to die. I searched high and low but could not find her. Two days later, she dragged herself onto the verandah. We took a last visit to the vet that morning, and I buried her next to Taz and Orla.

Taz was gone, Bangalory was gone; I was not a happy chappy. The evenings were dreadful. I needed to remedy the situation asap. I asked a farm manager friend if he knew where I could get a kitten. He told me his wife was in touch with a cat rescue group, and in no time at all, I was offered two ginger kittens who had been hand-reared after being found in an alley next to their dead mother. Male cats were not my first choice, nor had I planned on getting two cats, but the photo Theuns forwarded stole my heart. There were a couple of frustrating delays (rescue people good folks that they are, can be passing strange), but I finally fetched my, by now, four-month-old kittens on a rainy day in September.

Cisco is slinky and built like the Pink Panther; Nairo is thickset and looks like Shere Khan. They have temperaments to match. Cisco is laid back and very affectionate; Nairo is a thug but loves to sleep on my lap when I am watching television. He is extremely attentive when I am eating biltong. I think he can hear a packet open from the bottom of the garden. They are both vocal, Nairo, more so. They have both had the snip and are growing into beautiful big cats.

The downside of cats is that they are such killers. Nairo especially is a hunter-killer of note. If it was just rats – which they have pretty much decimated – it would be fine, but local birdlife takes a pounding. A Jackie Hangman haunts my garden, and I enjoy sitting on the verandah in the afternoons, watching him swoop down from his perch and dive headfirst into the lawn catching his prey. He spends only fleeting moments on the ground, and I was quite sure he was safe from the cats until the evening Nairo came out of the gloaming and caught him right in front of me. My heart dropped. Somehow Nairo fumbled the ball, and miraculously the little bird escaped in a puff of feathers.

Cisco and Nairo were meant to be it as far as cats go, but my neighbours moved and could not take their pets with them. I offered to take Potter, their black and white cat. Potts was badly mauled as a kitten and does not have full control of her tail; it bobbles at ninety degrees to her side or twists over her back or against her flank when she runs in a gait reminiscent of Korkina after her brain trauma. In her first two weeks at New Leaf, we never saw Potter during the daylight hours. She would only appear at night. As soon as the sun came up, she was gone again. I spotted her once; she was sleeping/hiding inside the plastic roof lining in the garage. She slowly got used to the dogs and the ginger coalition and is now very much part of the family.

Potter lives in her own world and is never still for very long. She often sleeps at the end of my bed at night; she also likes stretching out in front of the heater under my desk. Potter is usually the first cat to appear on my return home and will always give me a small cry of greeting. When I check on or feed the young stock, she will track my movements from inside the security fence and always be at the gate when I return. Potter doesn't like gusting winds or thunderstorms and hides under the covered side table between my recliner and the wall for the duration.

Cisco always swings by just before dawn, walking up my back or flopping down next to me for a rub and ear scratch, purring all the while. He is an excellent flopper. A quick stroke of Cisco's back, or the dampness of his paws, is my early indication of the weather conditions outside. Nairo appears when I make my first cup of coffee, ever hopeful for a treat.

There is a gap between the front gate and its upright, just wide enough for a cat to slip through. Potter uses it but never goes very far. Last winter, I would see her sunning herself on the round bales stored in the adjacent Kikuyu camp. Nairo goes further afield; I have seen him at the bottom of the drive, having just crossed the district road on his way home. Despite being neutered, I fear he engages in risky behaviour beyond our borders, as when he returns, he is absolutely knackered. Cisco has shown no inclination to venture beyond the gate, good cat that he is.

Cisco and Nairo and Potter have been the antidote to my gloom as I knew they would be. All the cats get on very well with the dogs and emerge from their hiding places to greet my return home, along with the hounds. Cisco has a bad habit of darting between my legs, and I fear one day I will be found lying dead and when they roll me over, Cisco will be found similarly deceased underneath me. There are worse ways of going than tripping over a cat. Being crushed to death by a large falling human, not so much.

Nairo and Cisco

Nairo

Sunday morning, stinking hot, we are all sitting outside; Nairo dashes across the verandah floor, head held high, a mouse in his jaws, and disappears into the shrubbery. I have to shout at the dogs to stop them from following him. An hour later, I sit at my desk working on this book when Nairo returns and proceeds to vomit up the mouse just inside the front door. The dogs inspect the mess but don't touch it. I fetch a roll of toilet paper and clean it up; fortunately, I have no sense of smell.

Nairo with mouse kill

Cisco . . .

the clown!

CHAPTER TWENTY

NEW DOGS

Dave Moberly and I were both looking for Bull Mastiffs. They were difficult to find. After we rejected some dodgy offers, Dave saw an advert for a breeder in the Freestate. We liked what we saw and ordered a pup each, driving up to Bethlehem to fetch them. Dave wanted a male; I wanted a bitch. Shirl Moberly named their dog Ozzie, and he has grown into a magnificent beast. I called my dog Aya. Aya reminds me of Major, the Pigdog in the Footrot Flats cartoons; she has the same broad chest, square stance, and undershot jaw.

Aya was incredibly challenging to house train – mastiffs are not the brightest dogs. She would purposely come back onto the verandah to do her business. Every morning the first thing I would do was open the blinds and do a turd check. A positive occurrence put me in a bad mood. It was months of expletive-ridden scolding before she finally worked it out. Aya has grown into a good-looking, hyper-alert dog and is Jango's 'wingman' when it comes to home security. She looks magnificent when she is in full display, tail up and all a bristle. She is incredibly affectionate, and if I am sitting down, she will launch her front end into my lap for a pat and a cuddle. Occasionally she does this uninvited when I have nodded off in my chair, and I crap myself; needless to say, she gets an earful. The mechanism that retracts Aya's tongue back into her mouth jams, leaving her with a centimetre or two of tongue sticking out, especially when she is asleep. I keep telling her it is not a good look. Her brother suffers from the same malady. Genes will out.

Determined to have two Bull Mastiffs, I purchased Shiloh a year later from the same breeder but from different parents. Shiloh and Aya are huge mates. Shiloh is a great galumphing pup with earnest eyes; she is currently in the destruction stage of her life. Toilet rolls are a favourite target. She also loves to chew on the toilet brush; they are now stored in the bath. Shoes must be placed at least a metre above the ground, or they end up outside in a state of disrepair. The nights are too long; at her worst, she destroys pot plants; lesser transgressions include bringing fallen weaver bird nests onto the verandah and tearing them to shreds or pulling half a dozen braai logs out of the stack and chewing on them. Just this morning, I opened the front door to confetti, overnight she had shredded two unread cow magazines I had carelessly left out on the coffee table overnight. Her favourite toy (as with previous pups) is an empty plastic Coke bottle (with label and lid removed). She chews them flat; I think she likes the noise they make when she plays with them as much as their chewability. Like Lexi and Aya, Shiloh will eat anything; leftover three-bean salad and overripe fruit salad all go down the hatch. When I open the security gate in the morning, I have to stand aside or be bowled over as the two mastiffs charge through to the scullery hoping for bowls to lick.

Aya and Cisco

Shiloh and Potter love the garden furniture

Shiloh and Jango

CHAPTER TWENTY-ONE

CLOSE ENCOUNTERS

I rep for a living, selling bull semen to dairy farmers. One of the worst things about visiting a new client is you never know what to expect dog wise. I have visited many dairy herds in America, looking at the progeny of the bulls we sell, and there is usually some strange looking hound named Moose hanging around the barn. The odd one barks, but only one has ever attempted to bite me, a young ill-disciplined Anatolian sheepdog on a Jersey farm in Oregon. My colleagues assure me that *voetsak* shouted with the correct inflexion is a universal term even American dogs understand.

Many years ago, I was in the Natal Midlands on a first-time visit to a prospective client. I couldn't find any management at the dairy, so I approached the house. There was no fence, just a hedge. Walking onto the lawn, I noticed a large dog sound asleep in its kennel. I decided that if I could get to the verandah without waking it up, I should be okay. I crept across the grass at my stealthiest best. Halfway across the lawn, and much to my consternation, I spied another dog – wide awake and watching me with keen interest, bright eyes shiny with anticipation. One peep out of this little bugger, and the brute in the kennel would quite likely explode across the paddock and rip out my throat. What did I do? Discretion being the better part of valour, I turned around, got in my car, and drove away. A faint heart prevented a possible sale.

I was visiting a farmer in Estcourt, the land of the British Friesland. It was not my first visit, and I knew they had two Dobermans but could see no sign of them when I entered the gate into the neat fenced-off garden. I walked up to the house. The front door was protected by a portico covered in creeper. I knocked on the door and turned around to wait, and there at my feet under the creeper were two sleeping Dobermans. I could not get through the door fast enough.

I was badly bitten by an employers' dog when I was farm managing, but the only time I have ever been bitten repping was by sneaky little dachshund who snacked on my calf as I walked out the dairy office; it drew blood the little shit. One of my colleagues was not so lucky; Gavin covers the Freestate and North West province. He was knocking on a Steynsrus farmer's door when a giant Boerbul bit him on the hand, resulting in a trip to the doctor and six stitches. A few days later, he fell ill and ended up in hospital, where they told him he had tested positive for rabies. Gavin phoned the office and his colleagues to say goodbye to all of us. He subsequently went to Bloemfontein for another test, and the count had dropped. He was sick for a week but recovered. The dog had been vaccinated for rabies the month before, and the only conclusion why Gavin had a false positive test. A very traumatic experience for all.

Still very new on the job, Trevor was sauntering down to the farmer's office – a rondavel at the bottom of the garden when he heard a noise behind him. Two Doberman's were closing in on him – fast. He screamed (his own words) for the farmer. Trevor's predecessor had told him to always carry a briefcase. He swung the briefcase, and both dogs latched onto it. The dairyman heard the commotion and charged from the office, bellowing at the dogs to back off. Trevor just about needed a change of pants.

Years later, Trevor was travelling with our boss in Mpumalanga. They pulled into the farmyard of long-time customers. Wade got out of the vehicle, and a giant Boerbul charged out and bit him on the arm. Panicking and with a keen sense of self-preservation, Trevor grabbed the passenger side door and pulled it closed with Wade still on the outside.

AC Kotze worked the Eastern Cape, he relates: "I am 100% convinced Ridgebacks have a breeding disorder, it is in their genes to jump up on agents, especially on a rainy day at your first appointment. I don't like them."

CHAPTER TWENTY-TWO

BEES AND SNAKES

I loathe bees; I will not pretend otherwise – they can save the planet somewhere else. Bees killed two of my dogs, and for years they have been trying to kill me. Every house I have ever lived in has had at least one resident beehive. I coexisted with three separate hives in the New Leaf house for two decades, all in the roof – one in the corner of the lounge, one above the spare bedroom, and the third above the bathroom. I always left them well alone, giving them a wide berth, but I was stung five times by the little pricks on one weekend alone.

In April 2008, I was judging a Jersey Show in Bloemfontein. Between classes, I checked my phone and saw half a dozen missed calls from home. Uh-oh. MaMtolo was verging on hysteria; swarming bees had attacked the dogs. Turk and Grip fled straight through the electric security fence surrounding the house and were gone. My two young dogs, the little runt Gooch of the big eyes, and Black Peril, a beautiful young Great Dane x Mastiff (Ziggy's littermate), were scared of the fence and had succumbed to the bee stings. They were in their death throws as we spoke on the phone. I spent a sleepless night in Bloemfontein, worried about my mastiffs. MaMtolo phoned just after 7.30 the next morning. When she arrived for work, the two dogs, bitter enemies, were sitting side-by-side, waiting for her at the gate.

Gooch and BP joined the other dogs buried at the bottom of the garden.

Grip and Gooch

Snakes have generally come off second best in this book, but they kill many farm dogs; my colleague in the Freestate has lost two Jack Russells and a Boerboel to snakes. The Boerboel had killed a Cape Cobra a month before, but its second encounter with a Cobra ended fatally for the dog.

I got home after dark one night and hopped out the bakkie to unlock and push back the gate because the gate opener was on the blink. I was talking on the cell phone and yelling at the excited dogs to get out the way. Suddenly I saw a two-foot-long Puffadder lying in the tyre track right next to the gate I had just opened. My heart rate soared into the red zone. The more I yelled at the dogs to back off, the more they bounced all over it, oblivious of its presence in their delirious quest for my attention. I realised the only way to remove them (and me) from danger was to drive up to the house. I hoped I had turned it into roadkill, but when I got the truck turned around and trained my headlights, it was nowhere to be seen. I shut the gate quickly and beat a hasty retreat. There was no whiskey in the house, so I ate three bacon sandwiches for supper to ensure the old ticker was well greased after the shock it had just undergone. Puffadders are cytotoxic and can kill a grown man, let alone the Bull Mastiffs or Jack Russell that were tap-dancing on its head.

A couple of days later, while I was out, my then two-month-old German Shepherd pup Orla wandered onto the lawn dragging a large snake. MaMtolo realised this was not a good combination and yelled for the guy fixing my roof for help. Conrad found a stick and approached warily. The snake was dead. It had a damaged snout, and his theory was one of the cats had killed it. I had my doubts, I suspect it was the snake from earlier in the week, and I had nicked it with my tyre, and it crawled off and died in the undergrowth.

Lockdown, as a result of the Covid-19 pandemic, has been an unusual occurrence for all. I have been very fortunate as cows still need to be milked and bred, and my business has not been affected. I did head out earlier and spent every evening at home rather than sleeping out. The dogs and cats loved it. Late one evening, I heard soft scuffles on the linoleum behind me; I rose from my chair to find the three cats lying on the kitchen floor, casually flicking a dazed and confused snake between them. I picked up the little Red-lipped Herald with braai tongs and tossed it out the window. This happened four more times over the following months; one night, I threw the snake out the window, but obviously not far enough as it was promptly retrieved. What gives me the heebie-jeebies is one of the cats' favourite routes in and out of the house is through a window gained by running across the back of my recliner. How many times was a snake hauled inside the house centimetres from the top of my head?

Last night there was more scuffling in the kitchen, and when I finally took a gander, Cisco had his head stuck inside my boot with Nairo and Potter close at hand, watching. On closer inspection, I found the snake had taken refuge in my footwear. It was small, about twenty centimetres long and very black. I picked up the boot and shook it out the kitchen window. From now on, I will have to check my shoes for snakes.

CHAPTER TWENTY-THREE

DISCLAIMER

It is Monday morning and not quite light yet; it is a month past the winter solstice. I have just let the dogs in. Lexi is lying on the couch. Shiloh is at my feet under the desk, enjoying the warmth of the heater. Jango and Aya have gone back outside after a quick check of the scullery for any dishes that might require licking. There were none today. Potter slept on the bed all night. The ginger coalition did not appear at all, typical for Nairo, unusual for Cisco. Nairo came into the house just before six, meowing quietly as is his want. Cisco only pitched while I was making coffee. To make up for this absence, he is now pressed up against my chest purring and demanding attention while I type with one hand.

It is a very early Sunday morning in November, and the sun has just come up; Nairo gives a tiny cry of greeting and flops down on the end of the bed, apparently exhausted after a night on the prowl. Potts is asleep on the chair, forelegs tucked under her chest. Cisco flops down next to Nairo. Everybody crashes for the next two and a half hours until a full bladder forces me up. I stagger through to the bathroom, take a piss, make coffee, and top up the cat's grub. I unlock the front door and security gate; excited dogs barge in, happy to see me. I drink coffee on the front verandah (watching my neighbours hard at work planting maize) surrounded by hounds collapsed back on their beds, except for Jango, who prefers the cold concrete in summer. Later on, I feed the replacement heifers and yearling bulls and walk down to check on the cows with Jango. I have to laugh; Shiloh and Potter sit side-by-side on the garden bench, watching my ponderous return.

Dogs and cats are a big part of my life; I am the boss, but they are my crew. They have always been truer to me than I have been to them. There are a couple on my conscience where my actions or lack of action failed them. Their lives are far too short. They cause such heartbreak when they die, but between arrival and departure, they are the very best things. Forgive me if you were duped by the tongue-in-cheek, clickbait title of this book; I highly recommend them.

CHAPTER TWENTY-FOUR

101 Reasons Not to Own A Dog – The List

1. Ball and Butt Licking – a notable skill rarely included in the brochure.
2. Barking – danger alert, but sometimes, the barking continues long after the threat passes. The danger can also be imaginary, i.e. nuisance barking.
3. Barkly – see Chapter 5
4. Begging
5. Bees
6. Billary – tick-borne disease, fatal if untreated.
7. Biting
8. Blaise – see Chapter 3
9. Bones
10. Burrowing
11. Bringing home dead stuff
12. Butt sniffing – how dogs check IDs.
13. Capnocytophaga Canimorsus – commensal bacteria found in dog saliva, and the reason why you shouldn't let dogs lick your face.
14. Cancer – number one killer of dogs.
15. Canicide – see Barkly and Blaise.
16. Cars – surely the number two killer of dogs.
17. Cats

18. Cows

19. Chewing – as natural as breathing for dogs.

20. Crotch sniffing/ goosing – Dobermans specialize in this.

21. Crocodiles

22. Crowned Eagles – see Maltese Poodles.

23. Digging – a symptom of depression, loneliness, frustration, general bloody-mindedness.

24. Dirty Paws

25. Distemper – vaccinate!

26. Dog allergies

27. Dog food – massively overpriced money-making racket.

28. Dog hair – see shedding.

29. Dog shit

30. Dognappers – evil bastards!

31. Dogs don't share – dogs are hardwired to guard their resources; they have no notion of equality.

32. Dominance aggression

33. Dominance hierarchy

34. Farting – dog farts are deadly.

35. Fetch – it becomes obsessive.

36. Fireworks

37. Fighting – see reasons 32 and 33 above.

38. Fur Baby and Rainbow Bridge folk.

39. Gastric dilation and volvulus (stomach torsion)

40. Genetic disorders – inbreeding reveals hidden recessives.

41. Georgia – see Chapter 19

42. Gorging – see Reasons 31 and 39 above.

43. Halitosis

44. Hamsters, Guinea pigs, rabbits, chickens etc. – dog fodder.

45. Heartbreak – see short lives.

46. Hip Dysplasia – don't buy from puppy mills and backyard breeders.

47. Hospital Bills – see biting and tripping hazards.

48. Howling – at the moon, passing jackals, car and house alarms, loneliness, for no reason.

49. Hunting – a death sentence.

50. Jealousy – dog's delight.

51. Jumping up – see mud and dirty paws.

52. Licking – see Capnocytophaga Canimorsus.

53. Leaking – spayed bitches are prone to this.

54. Leg humping

55. Leopards – both African and Asian species snack on domestic dogs.

56. Mange – skin disorder; see Ticks, Fleas and Mites.

57. Mud

58. Neighbours

59. Other dogs

60. Pack mentality

61. Parvovirus – vaccinate!

62. Poison – Temik etc.

63. Poop eating

64. Ponzi Schemes – there is always a new 'must-have' breed someone is trying to monetize.

65. Puppyhood – can last up to two years for large breeds.

66. Puppy Mills – puppy factories!

67. Rabies – vaccinate!

68. Rain – there is nothing quite like the whiff of a wet dog.

69. Red – see Chapter 5

70. Roaming

71. Roses – when puppies dig them up, it is puppyhood. When mature dogs do it, they are pissed off.

72. Rolling in dead and/or rotten stuff

73. Scooting – an itchy bum can be a symptom of infection, inflammation or worms.

74. Scratching

75. Sharp teeth

76. Shedding – dog hair, the serial killer's nemesis.

77. Sheep – natural prey.

78. Short lives – see Heart Break.

79. Shows – when pretty replaces functionality, a breed is ruined. Give any show ring enough time, and it will ruin any breed; it always has, and it always will.

80. Slippers, shoes, boots, couches, tv remotes, car upholstery etc. – see chewing and puppyhood.

81. Slobber – see Bull Mastiffs.

82. Smell – Old dogs and wet dogs smell bad.

83. Snakes

84. Snares

85. Sport – see Chapter 3

86. Stealing

87. Straying – there are few things more heartbreaking than a lost dog.

88. Tails

89. Territory marking – a benediction of sorts.

90. Thunder and lightning

91. Ticks, fleas and mites – see Billary, Allergies, Mange.

92. Toilet bowl drinking

93. Tripping hazards

94. Vet visits – traumatic for the dog.

95. Vet bills – traumatic for the owner.

96. Vomiting – dogs' vomit when they overeat, when the dead rat or bird they ate half an hour ago needs to come up, when car sick. For fun.

97. Worms

98. Yapping – worse than barking, much worse.

99. You are away from home a lot – a lonely dog is a terrible thing. Destructive too.

100. You are squeamish – dogs have no squeams. Nothing disgusts them.

101. You have no time – an ignored dog is tantamount to animal cruelty.

Aya

CHAPTER TWENTY-FIVE

DOG BYTES

According to Wikipedia, there are 498 different extant dog breeds listed alphabetically, from the Affenpinscher to the Yorkshire Terrier. There are another 56 extinct breeds – all gone the way of the dinosaur. It is always better to be extant than extinct. I have found sixty-two British breeds listed on the interweb. So, at the same time as the Brits were hunting the wolf to extinction, they were breeding and developing its descendants on an industrial scale. All dogs were bred to work; guardians, herders and hunters, even the Yorkshire Terrier was kept initially to catch rats. Modern dogs may wear tea cosies on their heads or live in handbags or have their hair and nails done once a month, but they are still hard-wired to be dogs and do dog things given half a chance. Good for them.

Australian Cattle Dogs – Car guards; their natural habitat is the back of a bakkie. More laid back than Border Collies, I'm not sure how bright they are. They can get pretty hefty with age.

Bassets – Not very bright, knock-kneed, foghorn yodel when on the trail.

Beagles – Not very bright, tend to roam.

Belgian Malinois – Greased lightning with teeth. Require lots of training and discipline.

Boerboels – Frightening bipolar oafs.

Border Collies – Brainy obsessive-compulsives, only happy when working. Not for town folk or the sedentary.

Border Terriers – Happy souls. Otter like. Natural affinity for mud and water. I have never seen a clean one or a sad one.

Bulldogs – Wheezy buggers.

Bull Mastiffs – Slobber chops. Good dogs that eat you out of house and home.

Bull Terriers – Garden sharks. Terrifying to strangers. Bull Terrier owners are certainly a cult.

Dachshunds – Disagreeable little bastards. Their feet barely reach the ground.

German Shepherds – Highly intelligent, highly excitable.

Great Danes – Imposing. Expensive. Relatively short lives.

Jack Russell Females – Best dogs.

Jack Russell Males – Kamikaze canines.

Labradors – Mostly inert.

Maltese Poodles – Small but often lion-hearted. The favourite prey of Crowned Eagles when Vervet monkeys are in short supply.

Rescue Dogs – Victims of abuse, neglect or abandonment, once they have learned to trust and love again, they are intensely loyal and loving and low maintenance.

Ridgebacks – Noble hounds when well sourced.

Rottweilers – Yikes!

Saint Bernards – Expensive to purchase, costly to maintain, require big holes to bury in.

Springer Spaniels – Water babies.

Staffies – All heart, no brain.

Toy Poms – Leaky eyed tap-dancing yappers.

GLOSSARY

Bakkie	light pickup truck
Braai	barbecue
Dassie	rock hyrax
Jova	injection
Kikuyu	kikuyu grass
Legavaan	rock monitor
Phutu	mealie meal porridge
Rondavel	round hut with a thatched roof
Tibane	warthog
Togt	casual labour
Voetsak	scram, go away
Wagter	guard, watchman

ABOUT THE AUTHOR

Paul Meade grew up in Durban on the east coast of South Africa. He matriculated at Weston Agricultural College in Mooi River in 1976. After two years in the army, he worked as a dairy farm manager in Southern Natal for fifteen years. In July 1995, he joined Groote Post Genetics (now World Wide Sires) as a breeding advisor and sales rep for Natal. He has sold over one million straws of bull semen. A Holstein and Jersey cattle judge, his passions are cattle breeding, travel, game viewing, movies, audiobooks, drinking beer with his mates, eating biltong and writing. He lives on a smallholding in Southern Natal, where he runs a small herd of pedigree Black Angus cattle. At the time of writing, he owns four dogs and three cats.

101 Reasons Not to Own A Dog is his second book, his first book, Dodging Cows, was published in 2015 and is the all-time best-seller at Creighton Farmers Agency in southern Kwa-Zulu Natal. Dodging Cows is a fictionalized tale of growing up on a farm in South Africa in the sixties, student life in the seventies, army conscription in the early eighties, dairy farming and the transition to democracy in the nineties.

Printed in Great Britain
by Amazon